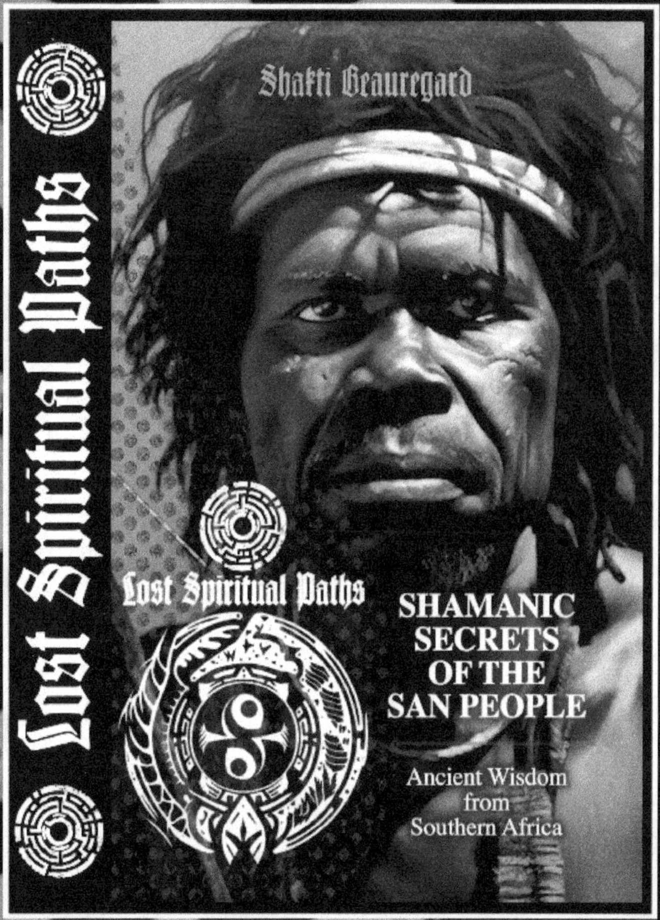

Lost Spiritual Paths

Shakti Beauregard

Lost Spiritual Paths

SHAMANIC SECRETS OF THE SAN PEOPLE

Ancient Wisdom from Southern Africa

Lost Spiritual Paths
Shamanic Secrets of the San People
Ancient Wisdom from Southern Africa

Author: Shakti Beauregard
Illustrator: Leofranc Maccari

ISBN: 979-8-89760-027-4

Publisher:
Beauregard Books
www.mythological.center
First Edition, 2025, A.D.

All rights reserved. No part of this book may be reproduced, distributed, or transmitted in any form or by any means, including photocopying, recording, or other electronic or mechanical methods, without the prior written permission of the publisher, except in the case of brief quotations embodied in critical reviews and certain other noncommercial uses permitted by copyright law. For permission requests, write to the publisher at the address below: mythmaster@mythological.center

Legal Disclaimer:
The views, opinions, and ideas expressed in this book are those of the author(s) and do not necessarily reflect the official policy or position of Beauregard Books or its affiliates. The publisher makes no representations or warranties regarding the accuracy, completeness, or suitability of the contents herein and disclaims any liability for any errors or omissions in the content. The content is provided "as is" without warranties of any kind, either express or implied, including but not limited to fitness for a particular purpose, merchantability, or non-infringement. The reader assumes full responsibility for how they choose to apply or interpret the material provided.

Neither the author(s) nor the publisher shall be held responsible for any adverse effects, injuries, or damages arising from the use or misuse of the information in this publication. The content of this book is intended for informational purposes only and should not be used as a substitute for professional advice in any relevant field, including but not limited to legal, medical, financial, or other professional disciplines.

Printed in the country of the market it was purchased. Please see back matter for details.

Written and edited in Africa.

Lost Spiritual Paths
SHAMANIC SECRETS OF THE SAN PEOPLE
Ancient Wisdom from Southern Africa

Shakti Beauregard

The Lost Spiritual Paths:

#	Title	Subtitle	Era
1	Shamanic Secrets of the San People	Ancient Wisdom from Southern Africa	Ancient times to present
2	The Ancient Wisdom of the Aboriginal Dreamtime	Mystical Paths of Australia	Ancient times to present
3	Shamanic Traditions of the Inuit	Spiritual Practices of the Arctic Circle	Ancient times to present
4	Forgotten Spirits of the Amazon	Shamanic Practices from the Jungle's First Peoples	Ancient times to present
5	Mysticism of the Circumpolar North	Spiritual Practices of the Sámi	Ancient times to present
6	Forgotten Shamanic Rites of the Siberian Khans	Mystical Practices of the Steppes	Ancient times to present
7	Mysteries of the Dogon	Star Knowledge of an African Tribe	Ancient times to present
8	Mystical Practices of the Maori	Forgotten Rites of New Zealand	Ancient times to present
9	Mysticism of the Kalash	Forgotten Gods of the Hindu Kush	Ancient times to present
10	Mysticism of the Tuareg	Lost Rituals of the Desert Nomads	Ancient times to present
11	The Mysteries of the Ainu	Forgotten Spiritual Paths of Japan	Ancient times to present
12	Mysticism of the Zuni	Lost Rituals of the American Southwest	Ancient times to present
13	Mysteries of the Indigenous Peoples of Taiwan	Austronesian Spirituality	Ancient times to present
14	The Shamanic Traditions of the Mapuche	Mystical Practices of Chile	Ancient times to present
15	The Spiritual Practices of the Bedouin	Desert Wisdom and Oral Traditions	Ancient times to present
16	Mysteries of the Polynesians	Navigators and the Spirits of the Sea	Ancient times to present
17	The Shamanic Rites of the Jomon	Ancient Spirituality of Japan	Circa 14,000–300 BCE
18	Shamanic Secrets of the Natufians	Forgotten Wisdom of the First Settlers	Circa 12,500–9,500 BCE
19	The Mythic Power of Göbekli Tepe	Exploring the Oldest Temple in the World	Circa 9600–8200 BCE
20	The Forgotten Rites of Jericho	Unearthing the Spiritual Life of the World's Oldest City	Circa 9000–1000 BCE
21	The Spirits of Çatalhöyük	Rituals and Beliefs of Early Anatolia	Circa 7500–5700 BCE

#	Title	Subtitle	Era
22	The Dawn of Egyptian Magic	The Forgotten Practices of Pre-Dynastic Egypt	Circa 6000–3100 BCE
23	The Lost Gods of Sumer	Unlocking the Mystical Secrets of Mesopotamia	Circa 4500–1900 BCE
24	The Ancestral Sky Gods	Tracing the Lost Beliefs of Proto-Indo-European Peoples	Circa 4500–2500 BCE
25	The Spiritual Legacy of the Mound Builders	Ancient North American Cultures	Circa 3500 BCE–16th century CE
26	Mysteries of the Harappan Civilization	Lost Rituals of the Indus Valley	Circa 3300–1300 BCE
27	The Gods of Dilmun	Ancient Rituals from the Sumerian Paradise	Circa 3000–600 BCE
28	The Forgotten Rites of Byblos	Mystical Practices of the Phoenician Priests	Circa 3000–300 BCE
29	Pelasgian Mysticism	Tracing the Spiritual Roots of Ancient Greece	Circa 3000–1000 BCE
30	The Elamite Mysteries	Sacred Rituals of a Forgotten Kingdom	Circa 2700–539 BCE
31	The Forgotten Gods of Ebla	The Lost Spiritual Path of an Ancient Syrian Kingdom	Circa 2500–1600 BCE
32	Forgotten Rites of the Red Sea	Mystical Practices of Ancient Punt	Circa 2400–1069 BCE
33	The Sacred Kings of Akkad	Forgotten Rites of Power from Mesopotamia	Circa 2334–2154 BCE
34	The Cult of El	Lost Mystical Traditions of the Canaanites	Circa 2000–1000 BCE
35	Mysteries of the Cult of Baal	Forgotten Rites of the Ancient Levant	Circa 2000–500 BCE
36	Mysteries of the Mystical Practices of the Ancient Maya	Forgotten Rituals of the Rainforest	Circa 2000 BCE–16th century CE
37	Minoan Mysticism	The Sacred Rituals of the Island of Crete	Circa 2000–1450 BCE
38	Mysteries of the Sardinian Nuragic Civilization	Forgotten Rituals of the Mediterranean	Circa 1800–238 BCE
39	The Chthonic Cults of Mycenae	Exploring the Underworld Beliefs of Ancient Greece	Circa 1600–1100 BCE
40	The Hittite Oracles	The Forgotten Prophecies of an Ancient Empire	Circa 1600–1178 BCE
41	Mysteries of Tarhunt	Forgotten Gods of the Hittites	Circa 1600–1178 BCE
42	Forgotten Wisdom of the Hurrians	Ancestral Rites of the Kingdom of Mitanni	Circa 1500–1300 BCE
43	The Zarathustrian Mysteries	Exploring Lost Rituals of Proto-Zoroastrianism	Circa 1500–1000 BCE
44	The Mithraic Mysteries	Forgotten Sun Worship of the Indo-Iranians	Circa 1500 BCE onward

#	Title	Subtitle	Era
45	The Osirian Mysteries	Lost Rites of Resurrection in Ancient Egypt	Circa 1500 BCE–4th century CE
46	The Mysteries of Eleusis	Rites of the Grain Mother	Circa 1500 BCE–4th century CE
47	Olmec Shamans	The Lost Spiritual Path of Mesoamerica's First Civilization	Circa 1500–400 BCE
48	The Sabean Rituals	Lost Practices of Ancient Southern Arabia	Circa 1200 BCE–400 CE
49	Mysteries of the Anasazi	Lost Spiritual Practices of the Ancient Pueblo Peoples	Circa 12th century BCE–13th century CE
50	Mysteries of the Sea Peoples	Forgotten Rites from the Shores of the Levant	Circa 13th–12th century BCE
51	Nubian Sun Cults	The Lost Spiritual Practices of the Kingdom of Kush	Circa 1070 BCE–350 CE
52	Scythian Sky Shamans	The Forgotten Rituals of the Horse Riders of the Steppe	Circa 900 BCE–200 CE
53	The Forgotten Rites of Sparta	Mystical Practices of the Warrior Kings	Circa 900–192 BCE
54	The Etruscan Mysteries	Forgotten Gods and the Secret of the Afterlife	Circa 800–100 BCE
55	Mystical Practices of the Hallstatt Celts	Lost Rites from Iron Age Europe	Circa 800–450 BCE
56	Forgotten Oracles of the Hellenistic World	Wisdom from the Oracle Centers of the Aegean	Circa 800 BCE–300 CE
57	The Oracles of Delphi	Forgotten Wisdom from the Temple of Apollo	Circa 8th century BCE–4th century CE
58	The Mysteries of the Orphic Traditions	Songs of the Immortal Soul	Circa 6th century BCE onward
59	The Cult of Cybele	Forgotten Mystical Traditions of Phrygia	Circa 6th century BCE onward
60	The Cult of the Magna Mater	Forgotten Mysteries of the Great Mother Goddess	Circa 6th century BCE onward
61	The Forgotten Fire Priests of Persia	Sacred Rites of the Magi	Circa 6th century BCE onward
62	Mystical Rites of the Sarmatians	Forgotten Spiritual Warriors of the Steppe	Circa 5th century BCE–4th century CE
63	The Forgotten Rites of the Druids	Wisdom of the Sacred Groves	Circa 4th century BCE–2nd century CE
64	The Forgotten Rites of the Nabataeans	The Gods of Petra	Circa 4th century BCE–2nd century CE
65	Shamanism of the Xiongnu	Forgotten Mystical Practices of the Eurasian Nomads	Circa 3rd century BCE–1st century CE
66	Mysteries of the Cult of Serapis	Lost Egyptian-Greek Rites	Circa 3rd century BCE–4th century CE
67	The Mysteries of the Qumran Essenes	Hidden Teachings of the Dead Sea Scrolls	Circa 2nd century BCE–1st century CE

#	Title	Subtitle	Era
68	The Bacchanalia	Lost Rites of Ecstasy from Ancient Rome	Circa 200 BCE onward
69	The Forgotten Gods of the Celtic Sea	Mystical Traditions of the Ancient Britons	Circa 1st millennium BCE
70	Ancient Irish Druidism	The Forgotten Teachings of the Tuatha Dé Danann	Mythological/Prehistoric Ireland
71	The Secrets of the Alchemists	Lost Paths of Transformation	Circa 1st century CE onward
72	The Gnostic Mysteries	Lost Paths of Early Christianity	Circa 1st–4th century CE
73	Mysticism of the Aksumites	Lost Rites from Ancient Ethiopia	Circa 1st–8th century CE
74	Mysteries of the Picts	Lost Spiritual Practices of Ancient Scotland	Circa 1st–10th century CE
75	The Manichaean Mysteries	Lost Spiritual Paths of Dualism	Circa 3rd–7th century CE
76	Mysticism of the Gothic Kings	Lost Rites of the Northern Invaders	Circa 3rd–8th century CE
77	The Forgotten Mysteries of Tiahuanaco	Lost Rituals from the Andes	Circa 300–1000 CE
78	Forgotten Rites of the Vandals	Spiritual Warriors of the Western Empire	Circa 5th–6th century CE
79	Mysteries of the Sufis	Hidden Wisdom of Islamic Mysticism	Circa 8th century CE onward
80	Toltec Wisdom	The Forgotten Mystical Teachings of Ancient Mexico	Circa 900–1168 CE
81	Mysteries of the Bon Tradition	Pre-Buddhist Spirituality of Tibet	Circa 10th century BCE onward
82	The Bogomil Mysteries	Forgotten Dualism of the Balkans	Circa 10th–15th century CE
83	Mysteries of Great Zimbabwe	Lost Rites of Southern Africa	Circa 11th–15th century CE
84	Mysteries of the Druze	Hidden Wisdom of the Levant	Circa 11th century CE onward
85	Mysteries of the Kabbalah	Hidden Paths of Jewish Mysticism	Circa 12th century CE onward
86	Mysticism of the Yazidi	Mysticism of the Yazidi	Circa 12th century CE onward
87	The Mystical Teachings of the Cathars	The Lost Gnostics of Europe	Circa 12th–14th century CE
88	The Templar Mysteries	Lost Spiritual Rites of the Knights	Circa 12th–14th century CE
89	Pre-Inca Rituals	Lost Mystical Practices from the Andean Highlands	Before 13th century CE
90	Mysteries of the Inca	Lost Rites of the Sun God	Circa 13th–16th century CE

#	Title	Subtitle	Era
91	Forgotten Rites of the Aztec Priests	Lost Rites of the Sun Gods	Circa 14th–16th century CE
92	The Spiritual Teachings of the Sikhs	Foundations of Sikh Mysticism	Circa 15th century CE onward
93	The Secrets of the Rosicrucians	Mystical Brotherhoods of the Renaissance	Circa 17th century CE onward
94	Mysteries of the Shakers	Forgotten Spiritual Paths of Early America	Circa 18th–19th century CE
95	The Mysteries of the Hermetic Order	Hidden Wisdom of the Golden Dawn	Circa late 19th century CE onward
96	The Secrets of the Theosophists	Mystical Paths of Modern Spirituality	Circa 19th century CE onward
97	The Secrets of the Akashic Records	Mystical Paths to Universal Knowledge	Modern esoteric
98	The Lost Teachings of Lemurian Crystal Wisdom	The Power of Seed Crystals to Awaken Humanity	Modern esoteric
99	The Mysteries of the Atlantean Priesthood	Rediscovering a Lost Civilization	Modern esoteric
100	Mysteries of the Ancient Astronauts	Lost Paths to the Stars	Modern speculative

Contents

Sunrise 1

Spiritual Practices of San Shamans 29

The San Vision of the Universe 59

The Language of San Spirituality 87

Shamanic Wisdom Through Time 109

Ancient Astronaut Theories and the San 129

Ritual Reconstruction 151

Shamanic Universals 183

Sunset 209

References 231

Sunrise

Greetings to all inquisitive readers and scholarly explorers. I am Shakti Beauregard, an enthusiastic researcher and chronicler of esoteric traditions worldwide. This text marks an effort to present a comprehensive overview of the shamanic secrets associated with the San peoples of southern Africa. They have frequently been called "Bushmen," although that term has shifted out of favor; the preferred designation is "San," acknowledging their long-established presence in the Kalahari region and other parts of southern Africa. Their culture has been documented as one of the most enduring anywhere on the planet, with a history of foraging, art, and ritual activities that point to a heritage stretching back tens of thousands of years (Lee, 1968; Barnard, 1992). Researchers have found Stone Age rock art, stone tools, and other remnants in territories that are linked to communities widely regarded as ancestral to the San (Lewis-Williams, 1981).

The heart of San spirituality involves a fascinating practice of trance-induction, sometimes referred to by outside observers as a "trance ceremony," that helps heal illness, restore communal balance, and offer contact with spiritual forces (Lee, 1968; Katz, 1982). This introduction sets the stage for an extended textual expedition into San spiritual practices and beliefs, spanning ancient times up to modern challenges and transformations. The content includes:

1. A detailed description of the communal healing rites carried out by San shamans.
2. An outline of the animistic cosmology that pervades San thought, emphasizing the interplay between sky, subter-

ranean levels, animal beings, and a variety of deities or spirit powers.
3. An examination of the distinct linguistic forms that give rise to specialized terminology—what anthropologists have described as a verbal key to hidden facets of shamanic knowledge (Biesele, 1993).
4. A historical perspective showing how these practices have persisted, adapted, or encountered obstacles through centuries of dislocation.
5. A look at speculative ideas connecting the San to "ancient astronaut" notions, focusing on celestial references or unusual imagery in southern African rock art.
6. A practical step-by-step example of a reconstructed trance-based healing gathering, offered in a modern context as a respectful homage rather than an act of appropriation.
7. A comparative analysis that sets side by side the San worldview and that of Australian Aboriginal peoples, particularly the Dreamtime understanding.

Age-Old Presence in Southern Africa

Recent genetic research has emphasized that the San might carry some of the oldest genetic lineages within our species (Tishkoff et al., 2009). Observers have long noted their remarkable capacity to adapt to the harsh desert environment. Traditional subsistence practices rely on a keen awareness of plant life, wildlife, and ephemeral water sources. Community members range across wide tracts of land (or once did, prior to contemporary restrictions), gathering roots, tubers, nuts, seeds, and insects, while hunting with bow and poison-tipped arrows (Lee, 1979).

Their homelands are thought to encompass a belt of the Kalahari region and beyond, although modern changes in land rights, ranching, and government relocations have eroded their territories (Gordon, 1992). Oral traditions mention that well before modern farmers and herders arrived, ancestors wandered freely, practicing these old ways of life without interference. Archaeological digs confirm the deep antiquity of their presence, indicated by engravings and paintings in shelters and on rock faces in present-day South Africa, Namibia, Botswana, and Zimbabwe (Lewis-Williams, 1981; Barnard, 1992).

Shamanic Realm of the San

What outsiders often highlight is the unique set of beliefs and rituals that revolve around communal ceremonies intended to resolve health issues, spiritual blockages, and communal discord. The word "shaman" is typically associated with Siberian or circumpolar contexts, but anthropologists have employed this term to designate individuals within San groups who master altered states for the purpose of healing (Lee, 1968; Katz, 1982). However, the San pattern is distinct in that many adults, not just a tiny group of specialists, might pursue the skill to enter these states. This broad-based participation fosters a social atmosphere in which spiritual healing is not restricted to an elevated religious caste but shared by a meaningful proportion of community members (Katz, 1982).

Core Elements of Their Ritual Method

Throughout southern Africa, the

bedrock of this practice involves rhythmic movement around a central fire, accompanied by singing, clapping, and the shaking of dried seed-filled cocoons or other rattles attached to participants' lower legs (Marshall Thomas, 1959). Women, and sometimes men, produce an intricate, layered chorus that evokes a sharp, accelerating beat. Within the group, designated healers or advanced practitioners exhibit physical and mental signals of trance at a particular threshold of exertion. The local term for this state is often written as !kia in English transliteration (Katz, 1982). Individuals in that condition become intensely aware of subtle energies they call n/um, a spiritual potency harnessed for healing (Lee, 1968).

    The phenomenon is not a gentle, relaxed drift; it often involves trembling, hyperventilation, even nosebleeds. The experience can be physically challenging, interpreted as a sign that the body is becoming a channel for immense force. Healers direct their hands or perform simulated extraction motions on individuals needing help. A sudden scream or outburst can signal the expulsion of malevolent force. By the close of the rite, participants often report feeling relief, improved relations with one another, and an enhanced sense of emotional release (Lee, 1979; Katz, 1982).

Broader Cultural Meanings

As part of an animistic worldview, the San interpret the environment as alive with presence. Creatures, waterholes, geological formations, and weather phenomena are viewed as participants in a grand interplay that includes humans, spirits, and deities (Lewis-Williams & Dowson, 1989). For example, the Eland antelope emerges in countless paintings and stories as a potent being with special spiritual force. Numerous rock paintings depict individuals with elongated limbs or partial Eland features. Researchers propose that these forms demonstrate how shamans see themselves merging with the Eland in trance (Lewis-Williams, 1981).

Cosmological accounts mention a maker or trickster figure, often referred to by names transliterated as |Kaggen, who shapeshifts between a mantis, an Eland, or other guises. This character might distribute boons or create confusion, underscoring moral teachings about moderation, community spirit, and humility (Bleek & Lloyd, 1911). A sense of open-ended possibility is found in these stories: humans and animals are said to have been intertwined in ancient times, and the present separation is somewhat fluid, especially during ritual states that break everyday barriers (Lewis-Williams, 1981).

Language as a Key

Another cornerstone of San knowledge is linguistic. The so-called "Khoisan" tongues have a phoneme system that includes numerous click consonants. These are often denoted by symbols such as !, ǀ, ǁ, and ǂ, representing a variety of click sounds rarely found elsewhere. The effect is a repertoire of vocal gestures that can sound surprising to the uninitiated (Traill, 1978). Words related to trance, healing, ancestors, or spiritual presence can carry specific tones or clicks that emphasize deeper layers of meaning. The name for the trance state (!kia) begins with a click that is itself absent in most global languages. The healing potency concept, called n/um or n/om in different dialects, likewise features these characteristic click sounds.

Historically, the San have relied on oral tradition rather than written records. This means that elaborate narrative cycles—about trickster gods, local animals, and family genealogies—have been handed down through memory and performance (Biesele, 1993). Elders recall extended episodes that can last hours around a fire, weaving moral instruction into entertainment, survival guidance, and spiritual reflection. Songs used during the trance ceremony often incorporate repeated rhythmic phrases that do not translate easily into Western categories of melody or lyric. Instead, they might be an amalgamation of vocables, occasional references to animals, and exclamatory phrases intended to guide the energy (Katz, 1982).

Challenges of Modern Life

In contemporary contexts, many San populations have faced dislodgment from ancestral sites because of government policies, ranching, mining, and changes in farmland ownership (Gordon, 1992). Several communities now reside in settlements or have adopted some measure of wage labor. Alcohol abuse is an increasingly destructive factor in certain areas, dulling the impetus for communal healing rites (Hitchcock & Vinding, 2004). Loss of land access and state restrictions on wildlife harvesting also undercut the underpinnings of a foraging lifestyle, which traditionally centered on small-scale mobility and a spiritual connection with the terrain.

These developments spark questions about whether the trance-based healing approach can endure. Some local activists and anthropologists argue that the practice needs direct ties to the environment and the old social structure. Others note that modifications—including partial fusion with Christian motifs—are already evident (Lee, 2013). Missionaries in certain places have tried to discourage older practices; in other instances, they have recognized that these ceremonies reinforce virtues aligned with communal support.

Spiritual Wisdom and Academic Study

Anthropology has played a role both in

preserving knowledge about the trance ceremony and in shaping how outsiders perceive it. Early European colonists often dismissed the San as "primitive." Later scholarship uncovered the intricacy of their worldview. By the mid-20th century, the so-called Kalahari debate advanced, spotlighting whether these communities were "untouched" foragers or had long been in interaction with neighboring groups (Lee & DeVore, 1968). More recent work has stressed that while the San faced countless transformations over centuries, core elements of their worldview remain visible, albeit in continually evolving forms (Barnard, 1992).

Potential Celestial Interpretations

A thought-provoking dimension in modern discourse involves speculation about ancient astronaut influences. Scholars in mainstream archaeology hold that rock art motifs such as half-human, half-animal beings or strange geometric shapes are best explained as references to altered states, spiritual illusions, or stylized expressions of a realm involving illusions not perceived in ordinary life

(Lewis-Williams & Dowson, 1989). Meanwhile, a handful of alternative theorists have proposed that certain figures with large heads or unusual silhouettes might be "extraterrestrial visitors" documented in prehistoric times.

While the academic consensus strongly supports a context of shamanic practice, it is intriguing that the same imagery can stimulate cosmic speculation in the public imagination. San narratives do incorporate star lore, with accounts of individuals who ascend to the heavens or an event in which a shoe or piece of hide is tossed upward to become the moon (Bleek & Lloyd, 1911). Whether these stories reflect literal observations or symbolic constructs, they showcase a robust fascination with the heavens. In any case, attempts to link the San tradition to "alien contact" remain on the fringes of scholarly discussion.

Why Examine These Themes Together?

A deep review of San wisdom, from their healing ceremonies to their star-related myths, can illuminate how humans across cultures engage invisible forces and the cosmos. We discover that the same individuals who track small footprints in the desert or gather succulent roots with minimal tools have an equal mastery of intangible energies directed toward healing. This dual competence—pragmatic resourcefulness in daily life, combined with an imagination that spans intangible realms—has drawn interest from anthropologists, psychologists, historians of religion, and spiritual seekers worldwide (Lee, 1979; Katz, 1982; Biesele, 1993).

Moreover, the San perspective points to communal forms of spiritual expression that do not rely on hierarchical priesthoods. Instead, many are encouraged to develop an inner capacity for trance if they feel a calling. The entire group is brought together in these events: some chant, some produce rhythms, some step in time around the fire, while others slip into a state that merges personal consciousness with energies seen as simultaneously beyond and within the group. This format reveals a dimension of spiritual democracy that resonates strongly with egalitarian social structures documented among Kalahari foragers (Lee, 1979).

Tensions Around Cultural Appropriation

In an era when "shamanic workshops" can be found in far-flung urban settings, questions arise about whether certain adaptations might exploit or dilute the San heritage. Many outsiders may attempt to replicate the trance ceremony without thorough knowledge of cultural underpinnings. Although curiosity is understandable, the threat of oversimplification or misrepresentation looms. Colonial-era stereotypes often depicted the San as simplistic or childlike, while modern romanticization can caricature them in a different manner: as mystical exotics whose practices can be purchased for a weekend's novelty.

Responsible engagement requires acknowledging that the San have suffered displacement, discrimination, and appropriation from more powerful groups (Hitchcock & Vinding, 2004). Any respectful approach to their spiritual tradition should involve recognition of actual community members who still practice it, or at least direct reference to genuine ethnographic studies. Royalty arrangements, collaborative research, or accredited cultural preservation efforts are strategies that attempt to mitigate exploitation.

A Look Ahead

This introduction forms the opening to a wide-ranging report that devotes substantial attention to historical developments, practice-based details, spiritual concepts, linguistic insights, and questions regarding the place of these teachings in the current global atmosphere. Through a careful approach, we can appreciate:

- The significance of these communal trance rites.
- The intricate set of beliefs that build the worldview of communities that live close to what might be labeled harsh desert conditions.
- The extraordinary variety of mythic expressions that revolve around trickster deities, shape-shifting episodes, and an interplay between life and death.
- The method by which orality, symbolism, and memory have preserved these teachings across millennia.

- The synergy and occasional conflict between the older ways and post-colonial transformations.

With these points in mind, we will then investigate the modern phenomenon in which spiritual explorers, from "ancient astronaut" enthusiasts to eclectic mystical practitioners, incorporate references to San rock art or ritual motifs. There is a certain tension between imaginative speculation and the cultural-historical evidence that ties these images to communal healing. At times, new theories can overshadow the voices of the practitioners themselves, who have repeatedly insisted that these paintings, songs, and trance events revolve around the living bond between them and their ancestors.

The final segments will offer:

1. A structured example of how a person outside the culture might set up a respectful "reconstruction" of a communal trance-healing setting, focusing on disclaimers and the need to avoid sensational claims.
2. A comparison with Australian Aboriginal Dreamtime systems, highlighting

convergences in animistic cosmologies and the function of trance or deep states to contact spiritual powers.

Respect and Rigor

It is essential to proceed with a sense of humility and thorough examination of sources. Although this text is written in an engaged style, I endeavor to anchor it in reputable anthropological and historical scholarship. Citations appear in the text (e.g., Lee, 1968; Katz, 1982), and a reference list will be included at the end in APA format. In the vast domain of anthropological literature, the Kalahari region has served as a key research focus for decades, giving us a solid base of studies on forager religion, symbolic art, and social organization (Lee & DeVore, 1968; Lewis-Williams, 1981; Barnard, 1992).

Readers might note that certain statements about "magic," "spiritual power," or "trance flight" may appear unscientific to some. Yet in the context of the daily existence of the San, these are not flights of fancy. They are part of a lived reality in which the entire group invests belief and energy. The feeling of stepping around the fire in the middle of the night, hearing multiple voices and claps echoing off the surrounding dunes or thorny scrub, is an experience that merges the sensory field with spiritual narratives. Ethnographers who have witnessed it firsthand often speak of the resonance it creates, forging potent communal ties (Katz, 1982).

Focus on Academic Honesty and Depth

This introduction marks the starting point for a thorough text. Individuals who read on will discover evidence from rock art research, such as the paintings in the Drakensberg area, Tsodilo Hills in Botswana, and other sites in Namibia. Those images, studied by rock art specialists like J. David Lewis-Williams, show complex arrangements of humans, animals, and seemingly hybrid entities that almost certainly relate to the experiences of trance specialists (Lewis-Williams & Dowson, 1989). Far from random decoration, these pictures communicate the concepts and visions that surface when certain men or women undergo physically demanding methods for contacting invisible forces.

Moreover, language data will be integrated, gleaned from the dedicated fieldwork of scholars who recorded texts and myths in the 19th century (e.g., Bleek & Lloyd, 1911) and also from the mid-20th century onward, when anthropologists collaborated with living elders in the Kalahari. The distinctive click-based phonemes constitute more than linguistic anomalies; they represent a code by which intangible knowledge is passed between generations (Traill, 1978).

Special attention will be given to the interplay between intangible beliefs and tangible social structures. The worldview is not compartmentalized from everyday life; it is part of the approach to sharing food, handling disputes, and forging alliances (Lee, 1979). The unwavering emphasis on egalitarian values, for instance, is directly tied to the notion that spiritual power is available to many, rather than restricted to a small priestly order. The group invests great significance in humbling the successful hunter through joking remarks, ensuring that individual success does not balloon into arrogance—an approach scholars call "insulting the meat" (Lee, 1969).

That ethic merges easily with the concept that the real source of healing energy belongs to something greater than the ego of any single participant.

Modern Implications

One may ask: why examine these ancestral ceremonies in the 21st century, beyond pure curiosity? For some, it is an anthropological fascination: how do small-scale forager societies function, and what can we learn from them? For others, it is a question of universal knowledge regarding states of consciousness: are there techniques documented among the San that relate to the global phenomenon of trance-based healing? Psychologists sometimes note parallels with group therapy, while neuroscientists might investigate the brain patterns associated with extended rhythmic motion and chanting. In other circles, spiritual pilgrims look to the San as part of a broader quest to reconnect with an older form of wisdom once found among many indigenous societies worldwide.

Yet, complications arise in translating these methods to a modern context. The lived environment of a Kalahari band—once characterized by daily foraging, frequent communal gatherings, and deep knowledge of local fauna and flora—cannot be replicated precisely in a city-based workshop. Even so, a respectful attempt to honor the spirit of the practice can yield valuable insights about how humans channel energies in communal contexts.

Comparison with Aboriginal Australian Traditions

In the culminating portion of this extensive analysis, I will direct attention to analogies between the San shamanic approach and the Dreamtime constructs of Aboriginal Australians. Although these two groups are separated by oceans and tens of thousands of years of distinct history, researchers have observed similarities in their rock art, mythic emphasis on shape-shifting beings, and the power of communal ceremony to reorder both personal and social well-being (Lewis-Williams, 1981; Elkin, 1977). The notion that primal spiritual outlooks share certain motifs across continents has long intrigued scholars of comparative religion (Eliade, 1964). We will see that the broad theme of individuals stepping beyond the confines of the ordinary self, guided by chanting or dance-like rhythms, is not unique to Africa but resonates across many indigenous societies.

In addition, the question of "ancient astronaut" or "ancient contact" arises in discussions of Wandjina figures in Australian rock art—another site where large-eyed, seemingly supernatural shapes have sparked outside speculation. The San and Aboriginal contexts often form part of the same conversation when popular media outlets propose exotic theories about extraterrestrial influences. Meanwhile, anthropologists argue that both sets of images reveal trance-based or mythologically grounded systems with roots in social and spiritual concerns, rather than cosmic visitors.

Organization of this Monograph

Following this introduction, the content proceeds through seven comprehensive parts:
1. **Historical Depth** – An exploration of how the San's Stone Age roots, visible

in rock engravings and older archaeological sites, connect to present traditions.
2. **Shamanic Ceremonies** – A full description of the central communal healing method, including the distinctive signs that a participant has entered a trance state, and the way the broader circle mobilizes around that moment.
3. **Cosmology and Myth** – A closer look at various trickster deities, including ǃKaggen (the mantis-creator) and stories about the moon, sun, animals, and the possibility of cosmic ties.
4. **Linguistic Features** – Examination of the click-based phonology and how a primarily oral tradition safeguards details across multiple generations.
5. **Modern Transformations** – A study of how these practices have been influenced by displacement, enforced settlement, wage labor, missionary activity, and changing youth perspectives.
6. **Speculative Archaeology** – A summary of claims about "ancient astronaut" connections, what rock art might re-

veal, and the mainstream academic viewpoint on these interpretations.
7. **Ritual Reconstruction and Comparison** – Guidelines for a careful, ethically minded re-creation of the trance-healing method in a non-San context, followed by comparative commentary linking the San approach with Aboriginal Australian Dreamtime philosophies.

Ethical Dimension

Before embarking on the full content, I must reiterate the ethical caution central to this project: the subject matter belongs foremost to the communities who live it. Anthropological and spiritual enthusiasts from elsewhere cannot assume total ownership or reduce it to a collection of practices to be borrowed freely. The impetus here is to present accurate information based on fieldwork, historical documents, and modern scholarship, while showing respect for the living voices of San storytellers, elders, and advocates.

Cultural appropriation remains a legitimate concern. The presence of a "San demonstration village" for foreign tourists, or an event in which participants pay to watch a brief version of the trance ceremony, can be seen as either an economic lifeline or an exploitative spectacle, depending on how it is arranged and who controls the narrative (Hitchcock & Vinding, 2004). By the same token, popular media occasionally sensationalizes the idea of "Bushmen magic," ignoring the real complexity. In writing extensively about these themes, my goal is to encourage an informed approach, not an exoticizing one.

Length and Thoroughness

I invite the reader to proceed at a reflective pace, staying open to the nuanced interplay between anthropology, history, and living spiritual traditions. Although many monographs on the San are academic in tone, I bring my personal vantage as a traveler and observer, hoping to enliven the narrative with experiences and insights gleaned from time spent with multiple communities across Africa, Asia, and beyond.

By approaching the subject this way, perhaps a new appreciation arises for how these communities have kept an ancient tradition in motion, even under severe modern pressures. Physical survival is obviously paramount, yet the intangible dimension of spiritual resilience deserves equal consideration. The San do not separate the intangible from the everyday. When a healing circle occurs, it addresses afflictions in the body, the group dynamic, and the spirit realm at once. By studying that approach, those outside the culture may glean lessons for their own contexts, whether related to holistic health, communal conflict resolution, or reconnecting with sources of meaning often overlooked in industrialized settings.

Final Note

This introduction paves the way for an extensive investigation into the ancestry, spiritual thought, linguistic nuance, historical resilience, and global interpretation of the San's shamanic customs. While the entire text should be seen as a single tapestry of analysis and narrative, this opening offers a glimpse of the breadth of inquiry. In the pages ahead, readers can expect to encounter discussions of specialized terms like !kia and n/um, references to seminal anthropologists and their findings, and a closing section that connects these insights to global questions of how humans interpret unseen realms, from the Kalahari to the broader planet.

Above all, I, Shakti Beauregard, humbly thank all those who maintain, study, and protect this knowledge, including elders who consented to interviews with earlier researchers. Their perseverance has permitted important traditions to persist, so that the rest of the world might better understand one of humanity's oldest living spiritual lineages.

Spiritual Practices of San Shamans

I have stood by many late-night fires in the Kalahari, and each memory fills me with a thrilling sense of raw vitality. One cannot overstate the impact of those communal gatherings devoted to transformation, selflessness, and mutual care. I remember first observing the rhythmic foot-stomping circle known among the !Kung Ju/'hoansi as n/um tchai. That term points to the special energy at play, but more than that, it refers to the entire phenomenon of a long nighttime ceremony of motion, group singing, and deep concentration on spiritual power. People there are not content to address sickness or strife with half measures; they rely on a formidable tactic that merges physical endurance, sonic layering, and direct contact with mysterious forces. Everyone has a place in that ring, whether they are the ones stepping vigorously around the blazing logs, or the ones clapping and singing in bright, high-pitched phrases.

My traveling companions and I sometimes asked the local healers what truly happens in those scenes, when individuals appear to tremble and shout, or even collapse in near-exhaustion. The answers were always couched in a single phrase: "N/um is boiling." As each participant steps in time, breath quickens, and the unstoppable momentum within the circle appears to open a conduit to another level of awareness. This period of intense bodily effort, leading to states of shivering or moaning, is not an accident; it is the precise route to access n/um. That word, which can also be spelled n/om, signifies a supernatural potency that is alive within those who train themselves. Elders teach that it resides in the pit of the stomach. Through intense movement and unwavering musical repetition, it rises up, traveling along the spinal column until it ignites the mind and body. In that fevered state, referred to as !kia (pronounced with a click at the start), the veil between ordinary sight and invisible realities shifts dramatically.

    I once spoke with an older gentleman, a respected figure in a Kalahari settlement not too distant from Ghanzi. He recounted how his father taught him to sense n/um as a young teenager. The father would have him run laps around a dusty clearing, chanting nonsense syllables at faster and faster intervals, then hold him by the chest and ask, "Do you feel it yet?" The youth would sweat and gasp, but only after repeated attempts did he finally break through. He described a moment where his legs tingled, the sky spun, and suddenly the rattle sounds echoed as if they were inside his own chest cavity. That was the sign he was nearing !kia. From that time forward, he knew the process and could apply it to help neighbors who felt unwell.

Even during these communal events, the approach is never identical in each region, and sometimes there are modifications in who leads or how music is arranged. In many !Kung Ju/'hoansi groups, the women form a seated circle at the center, although in other groups, men might also be part of that seated ensemble. They vigorously clap out layered rhythms and produce melodic lines in alternating high and mid registers. On the periphery, men carry out a stomping circuit around the fire, often wearing rattles made from hardened cocoons or other materials strapped to their legs. In my own hearing, those rattles create an almost metallic shimmer, though they are simply seeds inside organic containers. The combination of claps, calls, rattles, and footfalls fosters a wave of sound that builds until participants slip into something beyond normal fatigue. At that juncture, watchers might notice trembling, or occasionally a person letting out a startled cry, as if a jolt of electricity hit them from within.

  I once tried to keep pace with them for only half an hour, and I nearly collapsed from the heat and exertion. Meanwhile, older men continued for hours on end. It is not purely an athletic feat, although stamina matters. It is also about harnessing an altered frame of mind. The phrase "you move, move, move, until n/um lifts you" is how one anthropologist recorded it. I heard similar words repeated by a woman who participated in these gatherings regularly. She said, "It's not me doing it. It's the power in me that pushes me on." That sense of being swept along by an internal current is heightened by the unrelenting music that does not let you slow your pace.

N/um is the intangible force that fuels the healing objective. The group invests in this all-night practice so that sickness can be banished. In the local worldview, illness is not merely a random physical affliction; it often comes from negative energies or malevolent forces that must be confronted. A trance specialist, upon feeling n/um surge up their spine, gains extraordinary perception. They say you can look straight into someone's troubles, almost as if x-ray vision is possible, or see across long distances where no normal sense could reach. A man once recounted to me his own vivid experience: while in !kia, he confronted a phantom of a prowling lion that had been stealing goats in the area. In regular life, no single person would dare chase off a large predator alone, yet in that heightened state, he believed he could terrify the creature on a spiritual plane, freeing his group from the threat.

Healers move among the seated or standing participants, scanning their bodies or pressing a palm to the chest and the back. Often they simulate pulling something from the person's midsection. A flick of the wrist or an abrupt shriek might follow, signifying the harmful element has been extracted. Outsiders sometimes call this psychosomatic or symbolic, but for the local participants, it is real. Many times, I saw an older individual almost slump over as if drained from a fierce battle, sweat pouring down his face, tears streaming, while the person receiving the healing showed a look of relief and gratitude. Anyone present might say, "He took the dark thing away." This vivid demonstration of intangible forces being removed or cast out is consistent with the perspective that negative influences appear like a tangible poison in the body, requiring direct action to remove.

Sometimes the entire gathering is aimed at communal disharmony rather than physical illness. Individuals speak about resentment, jealousy, or anger among the group as something that can be manifested almost like a spiritual pollutant. Those old enough to remember the time before forced resettlements will tell you that it was crucial to unify people through these nighttime ceremonies. If envy or bitterness lingered, it threatened the survival of the band. Richard Katz, who studied these practices extensively, pointed out that the songs themselves awaken the interior energy in the hearts of the healers, which then pours out to cleanse everyone. The lengthy hours of repetitive music create a shared catharsis, so that participants can release any destructive emotions.

It is typical for these intense all-night sessions to press on until the very edge of dawn. Even if the group is fatigued and the children have drifted to sleep around the perimeter, the recognized leaders often say, "We must keep going until sunrise." One reason is to ensure no lingering negativity remains; another is the deep tradition that the transformation must be sealed with daylight. I recall once creeping away from a blazing fire around four in the morning, convinced that the event would soon stop, only to return an hour later and find them still in motion, though moving more slowly, faces shining with sweat in the firelight. Then, at the first pale suggestion of dawn, the music suddenly ceased, and a hush fell over the group. Several men simply collapsed onto the sand, breathing heavily. There was no big pronouncement, only an unspoken recognition that the event had fulfilled its purpose. Later that day, they might share stories of visions or glimpses they experienced at the apex of their trance. That mutual storytelling cements the lessons, passing them on to younger onlookers who were watching from the sidelines.

Although the rhythmic nighttime event is the most salient expression of San spiritual practice, there are other noteworthy rites. In certain communities, a Rain Rite takes place, sometimes including a mild level of that same altered state. The intention there is to communicate with powers that govern rainfall. In the desert, precipitation is life, so shamans will gather to coax or summon water for the group's benefit. Some rock art images show people in contorted poses apparently grappling with or capturing a supernatural creature that is associated with storms. I heard one local elder explain that this symbolic creature can appear as an Eland or as a hybrid entity. By defeating it in the spirit realm, the shamans let its watery essence pour down onto the land. She described it with absolute conviction, further illustrating that the San worldview seamlessly merges the practical with the mystical. Water is not only an external resource but a spirit-laden substance that can be negotiated with.

Rites surrounding puberty also have a shamanic dimension. A girl's first menstruation often triggers a celebratory circle that includes mimicking the Eland cow, sometimes with an elder man taking on the Eland bull aspect, thereby channeling fertility or protective energies into the girl who stands at the threshold of womanhood. I have witnessed women forming a semicircle, stepping around the young girl, chanting short, repetitive lines that reference the Eland's qualities—its grace, its resilience, its capacity to feed many through its meat when hunted properly. Some men might paint small designs on their arms or chests, or tie tokens of Eland hide around their ankles. Through these actions, they create a link between the physical Eland and the intangible spirit that fosters well-being in the girl's new life stage.

In addition, the Eland is central in other life events. The large antelope, known for its spiral horns and robust form, is widely regarded among these communities as having a special potency or life essence. This is why it shows up with such frequency in rock art across the region. Many paintings portray figures with Eland-like heads or partial horns, sometimes standing with bent knees or bleeding from the nose. Researchers interpret these as visual metaphors for trance experiences, where the boundary between person and powerful beast becomes permeable. I have personally stood in front of some of these painted cliffs, imagining how centuries ago a local shaman might have touched the rock surface with pigments to record personal transformations. One seldom-documented aspect involves divination. I learned that certain specialists can sense the result of upcoming hunts or glean answers to social dilemmas by slipping into a light trance state. Historical accounts from the /Xam, a group documented in the 19th century, mention individuals called "game sorcerers," who harness energies to boost hunting success, or "rain sorcerers," who attempt to shift weather patterns, or "sorcerers of illness," essentially healers. In more modern times, in Kalahari villages, a person might still consult a trance vision. If someone is missing, or if an important decision is looming, the community might ask a shaman to sense hidden factors. That shaman might find a quiet moment, slip into a partial !kia, and then report what they see. The process remains grounded in a worldview that treats the land as vibrant with invisible forces, and the mind as capable of bridging the known and the unknown.

All of these practices rest upon an animistic perspective, in which the entire terrain and all living things are imbued with consciousness or spirit. A San practitioner is a mediator, bridging ordinary activity and the intangible domain. The means of doing this revolve around physical movement, rhythmic music, patterned hyperventilation, and an extraordinary tolerance for discomfort over extended hours. Specialists do not ingest psychedelics for these states—an important distinction from some other shamanic cultures. Instead, the body itself, working in tandem with repetitive instrumentation and communal singing, becomes the catalyst for trance. This is why anthropologists often describe it as "classic shamanism," a tradition in which a trained person enters a visionary condition to obtain power from the spirit dimension, bringing it back for the good of all.

What strikes me the most is that their custom is not restricted to an elite. Many individuals attempt the training, though not everyone succeeds. It takes fortitude to push oneself to that extreme. In some groups, about half the men and a third of the women become recognized as healers able to harness n/um. This broad distribution of spiritual skill fosters a remarkable sense of unity. In communities that still preserve the older ways, it is not a single boss or priest calling the shots; instead, multiple people share in the caretaker function. If one healer is tired or ill, another can step in. This arrangement reduces any hierarchical monopoly on spiritual authority. I find that especially fascinating because it reveals how a small-scale society, reliant on foraging (until recent decades), might maintain stability. The burden of curing or exorcising malevolent forces is shouldered collectively, so no single individual is indispensable.

 I recall visiting a small settlement near the border of Botswana and Namibia. One evening, I saw a group gather around a modest fire after a successful foray for antelope meat. The men had also found wild tubers and a few ostrich eggs. While many were exhausted from the day's activities, an older woman started a syncopated clapping pattern, and others joined in. In a matter of minutes, men were on their feet, stepping in a circle around the crackling embers. From a distance, it looked like a swirling pattern, with ankles rattling and dust kicked up. I was mesmerized.

The euphoria in the circle built gradually, like a slow crescendo of breath and movement. Then, maybe an hour in, the volume of the chanting soared, and a few individuals' voices shrieked or howled. I recognized that sign: they had crossed into a deeper zone. One middle-aged man with a band of beads around his chest started shaking from head to toe, eyes partially rolled back. With his arms extended, he staggered toward a woman who had been complaining of knee pain earlier. He placed a hand on her kneecap, the other on her shoulder, and let out a heart-wrenching cry, as if physically wrestling with an unseen entity. When he pulled his hand away, he flung it forcefully toward the darkness beyond the fire's glow. The woman breathed heavily and then burst into relieved laughter, standing up to test her knee. That entire scene took perhaps a minute, but it felt like an eternity. Observing that was an unforgettable reminder that intangible energies, for them, are no metaphor.

Later in the same settlement, I learned about the concept of "star sickness." That phrase alludes to negative social emotions—

envy, grudges, rivalry—that can spread among community members like a malignant force. The rigorous footwork circle is not only about healing headaches or fevers. It also addresses psychological conflicts that might otherwise tear the group apart. The friction can accumulate if not purged. Those hours of chanting and foot-stomping allow people to vent their pent-up resentments in a structured, cathartic environment. The singing women, by producing certain repeated phrases, are said to awaken n/um in the hearts of the men. That synergy, they say, binds everyone together again. It is not surprising that daybreak is such a pivotal endpoint. The fresh light physically marks an end to old tensions, ushering in a communal calm.

Other older rituals are also noteworthy, whether they revolve around a newlywed couple, a first successful hunt, or the aforementioned puberty thresholds. The Eland motif returns again and again, especially among some branches of the San, because that antelope is revered for its majestic qualities. In old rock images, individuals can appear part Eland, part human, with unusual postures like bent spines or strangely elongated limbs. Researchers commonly interpret these depictions as a shamanic bridging of forms, or visual recordings of a trance-induced perception shift. I personally visited rock shelters in the Drakensberg region, scanning the faded ochre outlines of Eland heads emerging from stick-like human torsos. My local guide told me the significance: "They are changing. That's what trance does. You can take on the big horns, you can run like the Eland."

Meanwhile, the notion of divination rests quietly, less public than the main healing circles but still embedded in the tradition. When outsiders ask about fortune-telling or prophecy, many San individuals might shrug, suggesting there is no formal oracle like in other cultures. But in the words of one elderly woman from a settlement near Tsumkwe, "If your mind is open in the foot-stomping ceremony, you see who is hiding anger, or you see that an elephant is near tomorrow. You can see it." That exemplifies how the group's primary channel for supernatural information remains the same trance method. Some might harness it specifically to glean knowledge about hunts, weather patterns, or interpersonal disputes. It is a fluid skill, not necessarily separated into separate offices of "diviner" or "healer." Shamanic authority is flexible.

That thorough involvement of body, breath, and group synergy is reminiscent of definitions of shamanism from around the world, yet among the San, it stands out for its communal dimension. Certain Siberian or Amazonian traditions depict the shaman's venture as more solitary—one person in a dramatic state. Here, half the men and a noticeable share of the women can do it, generating a robust environment for shared spiritual support. Although differences exist from one community to another, the consistent features are the unstoppable circle, the scorching heat of the central fire, the layered music, and the final wave of exhaustion that doubles as spiritual triumph.

I have also heard of the intense physical side effects. People mention trembling limbs, nosebleeds, or sudden tears. These are all considered evidence of n/um's potency. In my first year of contact with these gatherings, I saw a friend of mine from the city become a bit alarmed: "What is happening to that man? He's bleeding from his nose." But the participants remained calm, only pressing a cloth to his face if required. They seemed to regard that phenomenon as normal, a sign that the spiritual current was coursing through him, burning away harmful energies. On occasion, a short shriek rings out in the darkness, startling novices. The older participants shrug: "He's fighting the evil." That direct and matter-of-fact acceptance of the supernatural dimension is part of their daily life, shaped by centuries, if not millennia, of practice.

Down through the generations, the pattern has proven resilient, though modern conditions threaten to erode it. Restricted access to ancestral land, changes in livelihood, and the infiltration of commercial or touristic exploitation can hamper the continuity of these gatherings. Sometimes, the communal synergy might be interrupted if outsiders demand that the local group hold a performance for them. The genuine impetus behind the late-night ritual is intimately connected to a sense of communal necessity, not stage performance. However, there remain places where these practices still flourish in an authentic spirit. Elders pass the methods on to the younger generation, encouraging them to keep the circle intact.

Even so, a large portion of the broader world remains unfamiliar with the depth of this method. People might have heard vague references to "Bushman ceremonies" but have no idea that these are carefully orchestrated transformations of consciousness in which men and women can see beyond the ordinary. In my experience, that oversight stems partly from the inability of many researchers to truly push through the entire night in the ceremony or to speak the local language well enough to parse the subtle terms. Another factor is the spread of monotheistic missions or official government policy that sometimes tries to sanitize or discourage what is deemed "backward" or "pagan." But for those who have witnessed or participated with respect, it is impossible to dismiss the power on display in that ring. The synergy of heart, voice, foot, and spirit weaves a tapestry that addresses the ailments of body and mind.

In some corners of the academic community, these events are labeled "trance gatherings" or "shamanic foot-stomping sessions." The name is not standardized across each San group, but there is universal acknowledgment that the objective is healing and unity. The older term in one group is n/um tchai, sometimes spelled a bit differently, signifying that n/um is activated. The best translators might call it the "medicine movement," though that is only an approximation. The real meaning is that the group's intention harnesses intangible energy. Meanwhile, the men's circuit around the fire is not a casual shuffle; it is a purposeful route by which body and mind converge on that radiant apex of spiritual sight.

A vital distinction emerges between the broad healing events and the more specialized ceremonies for special life stages or meteorological requests. Yet all of them share the root principle that the body in rigorous activity, matched by the voices of supporters, becomes the open gate to the unseen. This synergy is more than a pastime or performance. It is how the group handles adversity, protects itself from hidden threats, and supports individuals through transitions. If a child is sick, or if a mother has grown depressed after losing a relative, or if resentments have boiled over in the band, that communal circle can rectify what has gone off-balance. The synergy of repetitive music and bodily exertion acts as the catalyst.

The intangible realm is not far away; it is close, separated by a thin membrane that can be crossed via breath, sweat, and unwavering intention. That perspective reminds me of accounts from other shamanic cultures, but the Kalahari expression is distinctive in its communal emphasis. Everyone is present, from the smallest child to the oldest grandmother, drawn to the ring, warmed by the blaze, lulled by the layering of voices, and eventually catapulted into emotional release when someone staggers with tears or shrieks with triumph upon defeating negativity. The entire band emerges at dawn with a sense that the burdens of the night have been left in the dust or flung into the dark horizon.

At times, a question arises: is it purely psychosomatic, or does the healing truly rest upon intangible energies? Many anthropologists take a neutral stance, documenting the phenomenon without pressing too hard on metaphysical claims. Yet, the communities themselves speak of real energies, real spirits, and tangible outcomes. Some Western researchers, like Richard Katz, concluded that the process indeed fosters better emotional states, improved group cohesion, and at least partial relief from psychosomatic ailments. Traditional doctors who meet such events for the first time might call them "group therapy with intense physical aspects." But that underestimates the spiritual dimension that the participants regard as the core ingredient.

A friend of mine in Gaborone once said, half-jokingly, that if mainstream doctors had an iota of the unstoppable resolve demonstrated in the all-night foot-stomping ceremonies, perhaps hospitals would look different. I have often pondered that. Modern approaches can seem sanitized and lacking in communal emotional release. Meanwhile, the men and women in these gatherings commit themselves fully, showing how an entire group invests in another's well-being. This involvement is not a passive matter of watching from a couch. Everyone is immersed in the swirling dust and reverberating music, generating the force by which healing arrives.

Other corners of the tradition revolve around the Eland's presence. It can be the largest antelope, strongly symbolic of survival in a tough environment, so it is no surprise that specialists want to borrow its "potency." They may sway or adopt Eland-like movements when they cross the threshold into !kia. That visual motif has found its way into countless rock images across southern Africa. Some modern interpreters read these paintings and see half-animal gods, while local oral historians clarify: that is a depiction of transformation in the heat of the ritual. In turn, the frequent mention of Eland in puberty or wedding ceremonies arises from the desire to incorporate that potent energy into major life changes. The antelope's spiritual vigor is sought for fertility, endurance, and success.

Shamanic tasks also include the possibility of weather manipulation, with the so-called Rain Rite. One might see old pictorial expressions of capturing and slaying a "rain-animal," occasionally shown as an Eland, to release watery essence. The method described to me by an elder: the shaman enters !kia, locates the "rain-animal" in the spirit dimension, subdues it, and unleashes water onto the physical world. It may sound outlandish to someone living in a city far from the desert, but in these dry plains, obtaining precipitation can mean the difference between life and disaster. So, they use the same approach that banishes sickness to coax the sky for moisture.

    Shamans occasionally mimic the calls or strides of other creatures—lions, giraffes, or smaller birds—whenever they aim to channel that being's special qualities. It is almost a shape-shifting notion, carried out through outward movement. I was once told that the best healers can shift their voices to replicate an Eland's bellow or a lion's roar, bridging communication with the hidden realm. These examples reaffirm that the Kalahari worldview is strongly animistic: every creature is more than a piece of meat or a threat. There is a spiritual dimension to each, accessible in the trance state, which can be used for the group's benefit.

All of this highlights the remarkable tapestry of the San shamanic approach. The well-known foot-stomping circle is just one part, albeit the most visible. These people have proven that rigorous physical effort, group singing, and unwavering belief form a potent means of healing and self-exploration. Although many might interpret it differently—whether psychologically or metaphysically—the fact remains: it works for them. In older times, the entire existence of a band might have hinged on resolving tensions or curing someone of a deadly fever, so this method was an essential technology for survival.

    I have spoken to modern Kalahari San who mention that they still rely on it for guidance. If a crisis arises, or if a big question weighs on them, they might slip into a partial trance at night, humming to themselves, letting that intangible force rise. Then they can glimpse solutions or foresee a hidden obstacle. While the world around them has changed drastically—cattle ranches, motor vehicles, even government regulations about hunts—the deep knowledge has not faded completely. Some keep it close to their hearts, passing it on to younger relatives when they sense readiness. That is how it has endured across so many centuries in the desert.

Through everything, the image of that group ring remains vivid in my mind. People leaning forward, eyes half-closed, rattles clacking in sync, the heart-thrumming music rolling under the starry sky. The fire crackles in the center, illuminating the swirl of dust kicked up by bounding feet. Sweaty bodies glisten in the orange glow, and voices alternate between high-pitched singing and rhythmic claps. Every so often, a cry pierces the air —a sign that a shaman has crossed into !kia. At that instant, the wave of sound might intensify, as if spurring the traveler onward. Then a hush might descend when the shaman stoops to yank out the invisible poison from a sufferer. A final flick and a shout dispel the darkness. The ring erupts in renewed singing, some weeping with relief, others hugging their neighbors. In that moment, the entire group is united in a single pursuit: to push away all that harms their physical or emotional equilibrium.

After sunrise, each person's face shows the aftermath of a profound test. Some individuals remain utterly spent, yet they also radiate satisfaction, confident that their group is safe from malevolent forces for a time. After a bit of rest, they gather to exchange stories of what they saw in that intangible space beyond normal eyesight. One might claim to have soared above the huts, glimpsing a far-off well where animals were heading. Another might recount confronting a hateful spirit on behalf of a neighbor. Another might simply say, "I am empty now. The trouble is gone." In this manner, the tribe forges its path forward, cleansed and encouraged, ready to face another day in the desert.

In conclusion, the intense rhythmic movement event among the San is the beating heart of their shamanic culture. It covers healing, conflict resolution, mystical experiences, social bonding, and revelations that guide future decisions. Through repeated singing and strenuous footwork, they press beyond exhaustion into a zone where n/um bursts forth, unleashing a whole array of unseen possibilities. Within that zone, sickness is extracted, negative emotions dissolve, and knowledge from beyond ordinary perception emerges. The older generation invests tremendous effort in preserving it, and younger members take interest as well, though modern influences complicate the continuity. Nonetheless, it stands as a shining testament to a people who discovered that the combination of communal synergy, physical strain, and unwavering devotion to each other can spark an internal flame stronger than many external threats. If asked what has kept the San community together through times of hunger, displacement, or hardship, one might find the best answer in that circle by the fire, where sweat and song merge and intangible power surges up to protect the living.

Shakti Beauregard

The San Vision of the Universe

I often find myself marveling at the intricate layers of San mythic thought, especially when I recall the countless fireside conversations I had under the twinkling sky of the Kalahari, where people told me stories about ǀKaggen—sometimes referred to as Cagn—who is said to be both the Creator and a prankster rolled into one. Let me tell you, encountering that unusual duality in a divine figure was a mind-expanding experience. The older storytellers recounted that, according to the |Xam San of the 19th-century Cape region, |Kaggen could appear in the shape of a praying mantis one moment and then slip into the form of an Eland bull, a hare, a snake, or even something as tiny as a buzzing insect. In these narratives, he crafts the world, fosters new beings, and yet blunders in ways that prompt cautionary lessons. In one well-known tale, he supposedly fashioned the first Eland out of trickery and fed it honey, only for that creature to escape. Because of that, Eland eventually filled the human world, an event that both enriched people's lives and introduced the possibility of hunts, rites, and moral reflection. Some say |Kaggen's unpredictability explains why life is so full of contradictory outcomes: blessings appear but sometimes carry hidden troubles, or occasionally, something that seems harmful can bring a surprising benefit. This colorful figure is no static, abstract god. Rather, he is an active presence in the stories that shape the way many San understand the movements of nature, the nature of day and night, and the reason that animals and people each hold special powers. I've heard that among the Ju/'hoansi, folks also refer to dual aspects of divinity: a benevolent high deity connected to the sun's rise in the east, and a lesser or harsher power identified with the western horizon, the place of endings and death. That arrangement of the world, in which one principle promotes growth and well-being while another sows misfortune, underscores a recurring tension in their spiritual outlook.

Nobody explained it to me in the stiff academic terms we often find in books. Instead, everyday conversation was threaded through with remarks on how the rising sun might carry healing powers, while something in the western sky might hold the seeds of affliction. A friend of mine told me that his grandmother had warned him never to sleep with his head to the west, because that side belongs to destructive forces. I thought it was a whimsical custom, but they took it seriously as an integral piece of cosmic order. If a person fell ill, it was sometimes said that the lesser deity had found a way inside their body. Meanwhile, during a nighttime gathering for healing, participants might call upon the benevolent side of the heavens that commands rain and vitality. In older times, hunters prayed to the helpful force so that game might be available. They also strove to avoid angering the negative aspect, lest they sabotage a hunt or stir conflict in the band. Not all San groups speak of two distinct gods—some focus on ǀKaggen alone, or hold other variants—yet almost everywhere, one can sense a deep interplay of constructive and harmful energies.

It's not surprising, in that sense, that the same realm that births wild creatures, scorching heat, and fleeting rain can also hold myriad unseen presences. I often heard that the sky is the home of gods or important spirits, and that the movements of the moon or falling rain reflect their moods. In some ǀXam accounts, ǀKaggen resides up there, but at certain points, he tunnels underground. One old story from the Maloti area describes him descending beneath the earth, undergoing a change of form, and returning in a new guise. Older storytellers said the earth was more permeable in the early days: humans, animals, and spirits could pass through it or shape-shift without clear barriers. People didn't strictly separate the material from the intangible. In fact, those older folks said that in the very beginning, animals and humans were basically the same type of being. They walked together, spoke a shared language, and had no reason to fear or hunt each other. Only after a Second Creation did they assume distinct natures, discover customs, and settle into the present arrangement. That perspective on an initial fluid existence parallels what anthropologists describe in Australian Aboriginal traditions: a primal time with shape-shifting totemic beings, and later a shift into the current world's boundaries. The sense that we once mingled with animals in an unsegmented existence and only later parted ways conveys a fundamental truth about how the San see themselves: not as owners of nature, but as part of a continuum that once included animals as siblings.

Whenever I listened to accounts of |Kaggen's many adventures, I noticed a parade of supporting characters: a wife named Coti, a possibly adopted daughter or ward named !Kwenn (sometimes a porcupine), and a clever son, the Meerkat, called /Kwammang-a. The stories varied from one teller to another. In some versions, |Kaggen's wife scolds him when he fumbles a plan, or Meerkat outsmarts him in comedic episodes reminiscent of trickster tales worldwide. The variety of animal forms—Blue Crane, Ostrich, Bee, and so forth—points to a fascination with all creatures, each with its own role or significance. Ostrich, for example, might appear in a myth about stolen fire. Bee is sometimes the sacrificial hero that carries Mantis across floodwaters and perishes to plant in him the seed of future life. These episodes pass on moral insights: the Bee reveals bravery and selflessness, or the Ostrich shows both pride and downfall. In Kalahari regions, the Eland stands out for its unwavering spiritual potency. |Kaggen evidently adores that antelope, which is also the largest in southern Africa. I heard one story about how Eland fat is used in ceremonies around a girl's first menstruation. The fat is considered holy and is smeared as a mark of blessing. The Eland is believed to hold intense spiritual power that can be drawn upon. In old paintings across the region, Eland appear again and again, not just as a standard piece of fauna but as a gateway to a deeper sense of potency. The fact that Mantis is |Kaggen's favored form underscores that even the tiniest insect has cosmic importance for the San. There is an emphasis on stillness, on that distinctive posture that suggests meditation, which is why Mantis is seen as a creature of introspection. Some say if a mantis insect lands on you out of nowhere, it's an invitation to pause and pay close attention to hidden messages.

In many of these accounts, the spirits of the dead linger as active agents. A healer once told me that whenever the all-night foot-stomping event takes place, it can become a direct struggle with the ghosts of the departed. These ghosts, or gauwasi in some dialects, might cling to the living, causing sickness or disorientation unless properly appeased. Sometimes they help, but they can also annoy or harm. The notion of waterhole spirits, animal spirits, or trickster demons is also woven into day-to-day life. One older teacher explained to me that each significant place—particularly waterholes—harbors guardians that can either allow safe passage or bring disaster. It's up to local specialists, the so-called "medicine people," to navigate these relationships. The /Xam had a term, //Ga∂an, for a powerful spiritual practitioner. That term can be translated as "sorcerer," which suggests that earlier San recognized that dealing with supernatural potency was not always benevolent or harmless. I realized that in their worldview, stepping into deep states of consciousness is a serious matter requiring training, humility, and community oversight.

When it comes to describing the structure of everything, many San speak of layers or different zones that exist side by side. The ground on which we walk is just one region. Another, up above, is where gods, star beings, or the abode of |Kaggen might be found. Yet another is a hidden or lower region that can be penetrated during certain states. I recall hearing a Ju/'hoan elder mention "climbing a sinew to the sky" during an intense foot-stomping ceremony. That expression gave me goosebumps. Imagine breathing so heavily, chanting so steadily, that you feel yourself ascend through an invisible conduit. There's even a specialized term, //xoan, indicating that heavy breathing reminiscent of someone hauling themselves up a rope toward the heavens. Folks told me that a well-practiced shaman uses these intangible connections to reach above the ordinary. They might see the huts from an aerial vantage, converse with ancestors, or gather knowledge about the larger cosmos. They might also sense transformations in the night sky. In this sense, the cosmos is alive with personalities: the sun, the moon, and the stars, each with a backstory explaining how they arrived at their place in the sky. I found it fascinating to listen to myths about the sun once having been a mortal man with a shining head, who selfishly refused to get up early. Eventually, the First People beheaded him and flung that luminous head skyward so everyone could enjoy daylight. Is that not a startling yet vivid explanation of how the sun rose to universal importance?

The moon, in numerous tales, is no gentler. In one instance, the sun carved bits off the moon, leading to the phases we see each month. Another version portrays the moon as IKaggen's old shoe, left soaking in a river until water spirits froze it. Furious, |Kaggen hurled it aloft, where it became the faint disc that waxes and wanes. Such stories reveal an attitude that the heavens are shaped by divine or trickster actions, subject to arguments and conflicts. A friend in the Ghanzi region told me that her family believed a lunar eclipse happened because a hungry lion clapped its paw over the moon, dimming it so the lion could prowl the dark countryside more safely. To me, these narratives highlight how the San interpret cosmic events with reference to their daily challenges: a lion overshadowing the moon to facilitate nighttime hunting is a direct reflection of local ecological concerns. Similarly, that ring around the moon is read by the /Gwi as a promise of abundant food in upcoming days, a sign gleaned by wise watchers of the sky.

    The stars themselves can be ancestors, or they can be small creatures that glimmer overhead. One witty tale says that ants climb up each evening, transforming into those points of light, and then fall back down at dawn to resume life as insects. In older times, the /Xam considered Orion's Belt to be three tortoises floating on a log, while the Southern Cross might represent a few lionesses chased by male lions. Interestingly, the neighboring Sotho or Tswana might interpret the same star cluster in a slightly different way, referencing giraffes. Either way, the visual patterns overhead are recognized as living stories, intimately tied to community life. I find the idea that the Milky Way is akin to the backbone of the night absolutely poetic, and the notion that it might be the smoke of a great hunter's fire resonates with how integral the hunt is to the older San identity. If you stand under the Kalahari sky on a clear night, you see that hazy band arching overhead, and you can indeed imagine it as the swirl of smoke from some massive cosmic campfire. This vantage on the heavens is not limited to romantic stargazing; it merges directly with the notion that the dead abide there, or that animals that parted ways with humans still glow in the darkness.

    I recall meeting a blind man at a settlement near Tsumkwe. His words touched me deeply: he said that when he enters the foot-stomping ritual, he feels that "God puts my eyeballs back in so I can see." He insisted that, in that elevated condition, he can glimpse colors and shapes of the spirit dimension. He can detect who is in pain, which unseen forces lurk nearby, and what the group must do to restore balance. By day, his eyes remain unseeing. At night, in a trance, they open to spiritual truths. That personal anecdote sums up how the San unify mythic understanding with daily life. They do not merely talk about cosmic realms in bedtime stories. They claim to ascend there, in a bodily sense, whenever the foot-stomping event roars to its peak.

I once asked an older woman about the difference between these layered worlds and the normal existence. She shrugged and said there's no strict separation once you know how to slip into that condition. The line between forms is a boundary that can be crossed, just as ǀKaggen crosses from Mantis to Eland to Snake. She even teased me, implying I might be a lion or a crane in disguise. The fluidity is real to them. That is why older myths warn that animals used to speak with people until the second shaping of existence drove them apart. Yet even now, a link remains in the intangible dimension: the foot-stomping event is the means to rejoin them. So, in a sense, this worldview is layered, but the layers are not locked away forever. Humans can still roam them if they acquire the correct training.

For many decades, outsiders assumed that rock paintings were random hunts or decorative scenes, but scholars who conversed deeply with San storytellers recognized that these paintings are windows into the cosmos of shape-shifting, intangible travel, and mythic narratives. The Eland appears so prominently because it holds a central place in these stories. The sun, moon, and star references also appear in certain sites, though often overshadowed by the visual emphasis on powerful animals and half-animal forms. That is because the same impetus that drives a person to "climb" to the sky in a trance also inspires them to depict it on a rock face: it is an integral aspect of existence, both imaginative and pragmatic. Life in a harsh region—filled with scorching days, unpredictable rainfall, and a wide scattering of game—demands a worldview that sees both visible and invisible processes at work.

Countless myths revolve around ǀKaggen's doings, from the comedic to the morally instructive. He might benevolently teach the First People how to cook meat or trick them into a fiasco that reveals an essential lesson about greed. The Bee, Blue Crane, Ostrich, and other creatures either collaborate or clash with him, reflecting everyday life in the Kalahari, where bees provide honey, ostriches are coveted for eggs, and cranes appear as regal presences at certain waterholes. Each one has a story that underscores mutual reliance or potential conflict. Some versions portray Ostrich as initially possessing fire. Mantis swindles it away to help humankind. In the process, the proud bird loses its treasure. This instructs people about the preciousness of fire and the cunning that Mantis can employ. These myths rarely read as rigid allegories; they are free-flowing narratives told and retold, with variations shaped by local custom or personal flair. Such fluid traditions keep the worldview vibrant and personally relevant to each generation, rather than locked in a static scriptural form.

The advanced knowledge of Eland reappears in puberty rites, hunts, and even the foot-stomping that fosters healing. Eland is more than a creature of flesh. It's thought to radiate an energy that the healers want to harness. One story states that |Kaggen first forged it in some hidden lagoon and then used it as a teaching tool for his family, showing them how to treat this majestic being. The reverence for Eland fat in puberty events is intimately tied to the idea that the Eland's essence can guide a girl's transition into adulthood. From that perspective, the cosmos is populated not just by gods but by the potent presence of certain animals that |Kaggen introduced or discovered. Over time, these animals either parted ways with humans or bestowed gifts upon them, shaping the moral and spiritual ethos. The praying mantis is similarly exalted: some say if you stumble upon one perched silently on a twig, you must slow down, observe your environment, and open yourself to possible messages. The still posture of the mantis has led many to see it as a prayerful figure and an emblem of introspection. Among some families, a mantis landing on your clothing or crawling onto your hand is a sure sign that ǀKaggen is near, urging you to reflect.

Meanwhile, the invisible domain of ancestors and nature spirits adds another dimension to daily life. Many healers talk about how the foot-stomping circle can become a direct confrontation with the spirits of those who have died. If those spirits harbor grudges or yearn for life's warmth, they might cause sickness. On the other hand, if properly acknowledged and appeased, they can help protect the living. Some also mention waterhole spirits, intangible beings that dwell near precious sources of water. They might appear in dreams or trances, instructing or warning people. There can even be lesser trickster demons that create chaos in the band if not kept at bay. One older man told me that, centuries ago, shamans used to do elaborate nighttime gestures around a waterhole to keep its spirit appeased, ensuring the group would not be turned away from this essential resource. All this implies that a specialized skill set was needed to manage these interactions. The /Xam called a powerful medicine worker //Gaðan, meaning someone who deals with formidable energies. Even if a community was generally cooperative and open, it recognized that meddling with these energies required caution and expertise.

Many older Ju/'hoan or !Kung, when asked how they travel to the sky during the foot-stomping, respond with explanations that revolve around an intangible rope or sinew. Some say they tug on it, climbing upward, while others speak of a quiet whistling wind that carries them. The metaphors differ, but the idea of an elevated realm is consistent. And though the cosmos can be pictured as stacked—the daily environment below, an upper region for gods, and a lower region for hidden forces—these layers are not insurmountable distances. One can slip in or out if the conditions are right. In practice, that means that each nightly session can become a microcosmic recreation of mythic times, bridging the physical ground with an upper domain. So the star-laden vault overhead is not simply a random scattering of lights. Each sparkle might be an ancestor or an insect that soared up. A traveling anthropologist once told me that the San had an extraordinary knowledge of star patterns, using them to track seasonal changes and identify directions. They recognized Orion's Belt, the Southern Cross, and more. But at the same time, these constellations had storied identities: tortoises, log rafts, lionesses, or giraffes. Their worldview integrated the practical function of navigation with the narrative function of placing each star in a moral or comedic or cautionary context.

There is also an awareness that life is precarious. The sun can scorch the land by midday, leading to thirst and potential death. The myths about the sun's decapitation or the moon's repeated whittling by the sun express the ambivalence the San have about these astral bodies. Sure, the sun grants light, but it also brings searing temperatures. The moon helps travelers see at night, but it can vanish or be overshadowed, leaving the environment risky for wandering. Their stories do not cast these celestial powers as merely benevolent. They can be petty, moody, or aloof. That fluid combination of reverence and wariness is reminiscent of their approach to the natural environment as a whole.

All in all, one sees that the cosmic viewpoint of the San is not merely theoretical or reserved for a class of philosophers. It infuses rites of passage, daily cautionary tales, healing gatherings, and the practice of scanning the night sky. Individuals who have the skill might scale that intangible rope, see the "house of God," or gain cures or blessings. Such accounts can appear in statements from blind shamans whose physical sight is absent but whose spiritual sight, they claim, surpasses that of normal individuals. That is the hallmark of a worldview that merges mythic content with real, lived practice. A myth about the moon being an icy sandal can be told to children, but it also conveys that the moon's phases are cyclical, that water spirits can alter matter, and that IKaggen's decisions have lasting consequences. This is not an idle bedtime story but an explanation of why the moon shrinks and grows, integrated with a moral about carelessness or conflict.

In short, the entire cosmic system is encoded in tales that evoke laughter, awe, or caution. People refer to these narratives when planning hunts, consoling each other, or teaching the youth about the hazards of arrogance. If one stands near a Kalahari campfire, it's common to hear references to |Kaggen's mishaps and cunning ploys, used to illustrate a real present-day dilemma. A father might say to his son, "Don't be like the ostrich who lost the secret of fire," if that son is hoarding a resource or refusing to share. Similarly, a mother might remind a daughter that the Eland's calm dignity should guide her conduct through puberty, echoing an ancient story that underscores the Eland's place in |Kaggen's plan.

At the same time, certain outside observers might find it perplexing that the same group who see the sun as a beheaded man can also speak scientifically about desert ecology or track animals with near-faultless precision. But that is precisely the hallmark of these people. Their worldview is broad enough to hold pragmatic knowledge and mythic imagination together. They do not see them as incompatible categories. If you ask how the sun truly came to be in the sky, they might half-smile and say, "He was a lazy man with a glowing head." If you push for further explanation, they might add details about daily cycles of heat and dryness. The big stories offer moral guidance and place the environment in a living context, while the day-to-day tracking offers direct survival skills. They do not need to compartmentalize.

I once asked an elderly caretaker if he truly believed that the Mantis had turned a shoe into the moon, or if it was a parable. He shrugged and said everything can be both at once. The story is not meant to be hammered into a single literal or symbolic box. It's a testimony to Mantis's shape-shifting powers, which in turn remind humans that the world can transform from one substance to another, from softness to shining silver overhead. The cyclical waxing and waning might represent how resources appear and vanish in the desert. The trickster element also warns that even a revered figure can act foolishly, so people must remain vigilant.

All these threads of lore converge on the principle that their cosmic knowledge is not for idle speculation but for active engagement. The foot-stomping ceremonies let them ascend to the sky or descend below the earth, retracing the steps of ǀKaggen. The myths about the sun or the moon or the star-ants shape how they interpret each night's cosmic shifts. The presence of waterhole spirits or ancestor ghosts molds how they approach a new place, ensuring that courtesy and caution remain top of mind. The layering of existence, the frequent references to shape-shifting, and the comedic or alarming aspects of deity stories all feed into a worldview that is fluid and interactive. That is why one might describe the entire system as mythopoetic: it is a living tapestry of stories that encode moral lessons, environmental insights, comedic relief, and spiritual pathways.

A powerful memory: I sat one evening under a star-encrusted sky with a small group of friends near Tsodilo Hills. An elder started telling the story of how the Milky Way formed. He spoke of a time when hunters lit a massive fire after a triumphant kill and the smoke drifted upward, lodging in the sky. That smoke became a gleaming band to guide future hunters who might lose their way at night. It was a mesmerizing account. Then, the elder turned to me and said, "If you ever lose your path, look at that smoke in the sky. It's the old campfire, always waiting." That statement illustrated the bond between daily survival and cosmic wonder. The heavens are not aloof. They are a reflection of communal experiences, hunts, tragedies, and joyous feasts. Over centuries, the San have shaped and reshaped these narratives as they encountered new conditions or integrated them with personal experiences.

On another occasion, a local man explained that those who cross into intense trance might greet the old ones living among the stars, since departed relatives often ascend to that domain. A falling star, from that perspective, may not be a bit of debris but a soul returning earthward or a sign that someone has died. Indeed, 19th-century Cape San and modern Kalahari communities both mention that a shooting star might mean a person far away has drawn their last breath, or that an ancestor is dropping in for a short visit. This outlook is not separate from healing ceremonies or puberty events; it is enmeshed in every dimension of life.

In all these instances, the crucial point is that the cosmos for the San is an open book, but also a living realm that shapes and is shaped by human behavior, divine pranks, and moral choices. When the blind shaman said that God slips his eyeballs in during trance, it perfectly captured the synergy of myth and direct spiritual practice. On normal days, perhaps he gropes his way around the settlement. But in the heightened condition of the foot-stomping session, he traverses the sky, sees past illusions, confers with powers beyond the everyday. That direct interplay of myths with real healing or real moral decisions is, for me, the most striking element of San cosmology. It's not a dusty archive of old beliefs that have no place in daily life. Rather, it is an ever-present fountain of interpretations, warnings, comedic lessons, and uplifting possibilities. One can find references to ǀKaggen as teacher, bungler, and father figure all in the same day. Indeed, many of the comedic stories highlight that even a being capable of creating the Eland and the moon can make silly mistakes, thus ensuring that no one grows too proud or complacent.

I especially love how these cosmic visions blend with immediate ecological knowledge. The lion that covers the moon during an eclipse is not just a whimsical notion. It also underscores that the dark nights can be more dangerous for travelers and livestock. By assigning that event to a hungry lion's act, the myth fosters caution among community members who might otherwise wander out unprepared. Or if a ring around the moon is said to promise abundant gathering soon, it aligns with the real meteorological patterns in some regions that predict changes in weather or foraging conditions. It is a synergy that merges the cosmic dimension with local survival strategies, forging an unbroken circle of meaning. So to immerse yourself in San cosmology is to find yourself standing on earth with eyes turned skyward, sensing that each gust of wind or each flicker of starlight conveys some layered message. This is not about worshipping random forces but about living in an environment replete with playful, dangerous, or protective energies. And if someone asks how the Universe is structured, the answer might come in a story about Mantis forging an Eland in a hidden pool, or about the sun being a decapitated man's head, or about how you can climb a sinew to the gods in a night's ceremony if you have the training.

These accounts do more than entertain. They shape how you greet dawn, how you relate to an insect perched on a twig, how you respond to a shooting star, how you interpret your neighbor's sickness, and how you see your own place in the grand scheme of things. It's an all-encompassing framework, yet it remains fluid, open to retelling, comedic twists, and expansions when new experiences arise. In reading about |Kaggen, one might laugh at the absurdities but also feel the weight of moral reflection: if even the Great Maker can act foolishly, then humans certainly must be careful. If the moon might be turned from a shoe to a silver disc, then maybe anything in life can transform with an unexpected push. This sense of infinite possibility permeates daily life in many San communities. They hold dear that sense that the Universe is alive, storied, and accessible. They hold it not as an abstract set of theories, but as a tapestry of comedic, sometimes dark, sometimes wondrous tales that they actively breathe into every foot-stomp, every hunt, every moment of scanning the horizon for a potential rain cloud or a lurking predator.

Having journeyed among them, I keep those images close to my heart: the fluid shape-shifting of IKaggen, the massive Eland's spiritual aura, the meltdown of a shoe into a lunar disc, the idea that humans and animals once shared a bond that was only parted in some second act of creation, and the notion that ancestors are shimmering above. It's a worldview that encourages humility, creativity, and communal care. It allows for comedic accounts of divine bungling, but never loses sight of the precious knowledge required to survive and even thrive in a challenging environment. That synergy, that sense of myth as a living force, is what makes San cosmology so exhilarating to me. And it's also what merges seamlessly with their healing traditions: that cosmic perspective undergirds the foot-stomping nights, the presence of Mantis as a guide, and the ability to climb intangible routes to see the face of God. In that sense, every event in daily life is potentially part of the cosmic dance, or at least an invitation to remember how |Kaggen once stumbled and then soared. And so the stories continue in each firelit circle under that luminous African sky, where the Milky Way's haze glows like a silent tribute to ancient hunts, comedic tricksters, and the hearts of ancestors.

The Language of San Spirituality

I recall sitting with a San elder in the late afternoon sun, hearing her speak in a language whose very sounds seemed alive, punctuated by rhythmic clicks that kept my ears attuned to every syllable. It felt as if each expression carried layers of power and subtlety, woven through with clicks and tonal shifts that few outsiders could reproduce. It is often stated that these so-called "Khoisan" tongues, such as ǀXam, !Xũ, Ju/'hoan, Naro, or !Xóõ, rank among the planet's most phonetically multifaceted. One can hear a speaker say the word "!kia" for the trance condition, and that initial click alone captures a depth of meaning: it sparks the imagination, symbolizing a doorway to another realm. That impression remained with me long after I said goodbye to that community, because it illuminated the fact that these languages are more than just tools for daily conversation. They embody spiritual traditions, encoded in onomatopoeic or symbolic ways that keep ancient wisdom fresh.

The reverence the San have for their speech is unmistakable. Without a written script older than the 19th-century archival efforts, these folks have passed sacred narratives across generations purely by word of mouth. Young ones learn the old stories by hearing them repeated around fires or at gatherings; there is no dusty library that they reference. Instead, each elder becomes a walking repository of lore, safeguarding myths, songs, moral lessons, and practical know-how. In many cultures, that might feel precarious, but here, it is a longstanding process that has nurtured continuity for centuries. Imagine that for thousands of years, these communities have carried entire epics in their minds, maintaining precise lexical forms, with clicks and tones shifting only gradually over the centuries.

One might speculate that these languages, peppered with distinctive clicks, align with the environment. Some anthropologists suggest that the repeated consonants mirror calls of desert birds or echoes of animal footfalls. Whether that is literally the case or just romantic speculation, it's undeniable that the languages reflect a tight bond with the desert surroundings. I remember hearing a group of women singing a repetitive refrain during a foot-stomping circle at dusk, and portions of their chant sounded reminiscent of wind gusts across thorny shrubs. Others sounded like staccato clicks a small bird might produce near waterholes. Even though the exact textual meaning of the chant was sometimes intangible—perhaps just vocables—everyone recognized it as spiritually significant, an inherited formula that awakened the group's shamanic core.

N/um and !kia are two prime examples of terms that carry a spiritual weight untranslatable in full. One might call n/um an energy or medicine power, but that only scrapes the surface of its breadth. The word references the vital spark that courses through healers and certain plants, a type of interior fire that can be ignited by physical exertion and communal singing. In older /Xam usage, a cognate for n/um was gauwa, meaning supernatural potency. Present-day Ju/'hoansi might say n/um kxao—"owners of n/um"—to identify recognized healers. The linguistic link between n/um and words for nourishment or fuel underscores that in the San worldview, this intangible presence must be "burned" inside the body to achieve the altered state. I can still see the dancing men (though "foot-stomping" is perhaps a more accurate phrase) describing the sensation of n/um rising from their bellies to their chests, culminating in a trembling in the skull. They always used that distinctive word, n/um, with an air of awe.

Meanwhile, !kia (or sometimes spelled !aia, or pronounced with variations) names that half-death condition the healers enter. The expression might be said to hold connotations of passing through intense pain or crossing the barrier between bodily existence and the spiritual plane. When a San says "I have !kia," it means they've reached the pinnacle of shamanic achievement: they can see inside bodies, speak to the departed, fling out evil, or harness the Eland's potency. In daily English, calling it a trance might capture a fragment of the reality, but the emotional and physical layers embedded in the click-laden "!kia" are lost. The language itself, with that abrupt click, dramatizes the shift away from regular consciousness. I once tried pronouncing it under the guidance of a Ju/'hoan speaker, and she corrected me multiple times until my mouth could produce the lateral click with the right aspiration. She said the word must bite the air, must be felt in the side of the tongue, or the effect is incomplete.

No discussion of these tongues would be complete without mentioning how the names of mythic figures and deities also reveal a fusion of the everyday with the divine. Kaggen or Cagn, the Mantis deity in /Xam, literally stems from the word for the praying mantis insect. That means a mundane creature's name is also the name of the shape-shifting trickster-creator. In speech, there is less separation between the insect realm and cosmic narrative. Another example might be /Kwammang-a (Meerkat) or //Kaulǀna (Great Anteater), names that unify the natural world with the supernatural domain. Animals and gods blend in the lexicon, just as they do in painting or stories. I've pondered the effect on conceptual thinking: if a single lexical item stands for a small insect in the bush but also for a cosmic meddler who helped shape the world, that might encourage a dynamic perspective on reality.

I find it stirring that the Ju/'hoan phrase n!ore indicates an ancestral homeland that is not merely a physical place but also a fountain of identity, nourishment, and spirit. That term resonates with how certain elders said, "Our n!ore is who we are," capturing the sense that the land itself is integral to their being. An outside observer might talk about territory in purely geopolitical terms, but for a Ju/'hoan speaker, land is inseparable from memory, from the intangible presence of forebears, from the practical knowledge of water sources, and from the moral obligations of communal sharing. In older times, losing n!ore could mean losing a piece of one's soul. The fact that this concept has its own special label in the language underscores a worldview that defies simplistic translations.

When we look at the distinction between a major foot-stomping circle and a quieter session by the home fire, we discover that the Ju/'hoan phrase g//aoa indicates a more low-key healing chant, distinct from the climactic all-night rite. I find it remarkable that so many specialized words exist to differentiate levels of ritual intensity. Another term, //an, can signify a calling or a beckoning that someone hears from afar, compelling them to join in. Such specificity is typical in these languages, reflecting a refined sensitivity to different contexts of communal spirituality. That is the beauty of a purely oral tradition: the impetus to maintain exact shades of meaning. In a written culture, it is easier to say, "We'll use the same word in writing, and folks will interpret it from context." But in a purely spoken environment, every nuance helps keep references crystal clear.

The /Xam people famously provided a wealth of oral literature to the researchers Bleek and Lloyd in the 19th century, and those transcripts still amaze linguists. These storytellers recounted hour-long narratives that encompassed genealogical details, hunting tips, cosmic speculation, and moral lessons. The consistency with which they used certain terms to describe intangible concepts is astonishing, given that not one word was written down by the storytellers themselves; it was all in memory. People would clarify the layered meanings behind single words, pointing out that "water" might also mean "fortune," or that "heart" is akin to "courage." That pairing of physical and abstract senses in one lexical root indicates a deep metaphorical approach to life. Even the phrase for a formal greeting, //khabu ai ǁ'ausi, roughly translating as "I see you," extends beyond mere politeness, implying that one recognizes the deeper presence in the other person.

Symbolic statements abound in these tongues, especially when describing spiritual encounters. A shaman might return from a vigorous foot-stomping event and say, "I have died." This would not be taken as literal but as a poetic truth capturing the dissolution of the self that happens in full !kia. Another might claim, "I have changed into an Eland," indicating that she felt the presence of that powerful animal surging within her. Outsiders hearing such lines might assume it's some random exaggeration, but in context, it is a natural expression of intangible experience. The same rhetorical style can be found in the deeper mythical constructs: "First Creation," or g=ai n!gaing!ani, denotes that primeval era when humans and animals shared identities, whereas "Second Creation," or g!xoa, means the dividing line was drawn, introducing speech as the key factor that shaped present reality. In that sense, language itself is a divine gift, a magical threshold that reorganized existence. The story goes that in the earliest days, there was no difference between beasts and people, but once words emerged, boundaries formed, and each group acquired distinct forms. That myth alone suggests how strongly the San regard language as the root of civilization. They see it not as a casual tool but as the seed of order and identity.

Such devotion to linguistic subtlety extends into philosophical expressions of group identity. I love the pairing of "circle people" (=ahmi khoe) for themselves and "straight line people" (!huijuasi) for outsiders who are perceived as living in a more rigid, linear way. It captures not just a difference in custom but a deeper rift in outlook. Circle people revolve around communal gathering, cyclical tasks, and reciprocity in hunts. Straight line people build fences, follow strict timetables, and chase after property with minimal regard for cyclical rhythms. A single lexical distinction communicates an entire worldview. I recall some younger San explaining to me how they felt torn between wanting to remain circle people at heart but being forced by modern schooling or wage labor to adopt linear habits. The language gave them a quick way to articulate that cultural tension.

In addition, these tongues flow seamlessly into song and chant. A large segment of the communal foot-stomping event is shaped by repeated syllables, sometimes described as nonsense words. Yet those syllables are revered as gifts from the spirit realm, or from the earliest ancestors. The so-called "Giraffe Song" in !Kung tradition is one example, used in healing ceremonies. The verses may not carry literal narratives, but they hold powerful vibrations that feed the rising energy of n/um. Singers claim these patterns were transmitted from older times, and by chanting them, one calls on those potent roots. The fact that these languages are tonal or have pitch variations means that the chant can slip between speech and melody almost seamlessly, reinforcing the sense of a unified spiritual environment.

When we recognize that the San languages handle so many intangible dimensions, we see how vital it is that they remain living traditions. Unfortunately, modern circumstances place them at risk. Many younger individuals have grown up speaking dominant tongues like Setswana or Afrikaans, encountering daily life in towns or villages where the old clicks are less common. This shift can lead to a rapid decline in intergenerational transmission. Elders lament that if fewer people speak the language, the spiritual potency coded in words like n!ore, g//aoa, or n/um might weaken. If the precise click for "trance" is lost, the impetus for the foot-stomping circle might also fade. Language is the anchor holding the intangible realm in place. I recall a teacher lamenting that "Some of our youth no longer feel the call of !kia, because they do not hear or speak these words from birth." That statement suggests a profound link between daily speech and the capacity to engage with the spiritual domain.

The memory feats required to sustain orality are breathtaking. Elders recall genealogies many generations deep, along with lore about hunts, moral tales involving tricksters, and instructions for building good social relations. They do so without the benefit of any written record. Indeed, in the mid-1800s, when Bleek and Lloyd were painstakingly transcribing /Xam narratives, they discovered that each informant could recite hours of mythic episodes verbatim. They also discovered that subtle lexical items had multiple layers of meaning, so the scholars had to provide footnotes to capture the complexity. Consider the greeting phrase that references seeing not just a physical presence but the intangible aura of a person. The same logic applies to a word for water that might also mean luck. This reveals a synesthetic approach to language, where the physical merges with the spiritual in the same signifier.

When a modern researcher tries to interpret a short phrase uttered by a shaman in the midst of a foot-stomping event, they might initially think it a random exclamation. But those few syllables, shaped by clicks, might be calling upon an entire reservoir of mythic references, perhaps an archaic invocation that traces back centuries. This is why it's so easy to misunderstand the rhetorical power of these languages if one only relies on superficial translations. The performance aspect is crucial. A phrase might shift in meaning depending on whether it is spoken in a calm voice or chanted at the height of n/um ignition. A single click, placed differently, can alter the nuance from summoning a spirit to denouncing an evil presence. Observers who do not grasp that distinction might record the same expression for both contexts, losing the essential difference.

I have seen that the most advanced healers treat language itself as a kind of living force, akin to a bridge linking flesh and spirit. One older man told me, "If I cannot speak it, I cannot walk there." By that, he implied that naming certain spiritual states or calling upon certain ancestral resources must be done with the precise words. If the correct lexical item is not used, or if the clicks are mispronounced, the path remains closed. That is an oral articulation of the worldview that "speech is the second creation," the act that divides chaos from order. It resonates with the idea that humans and animals parted ways once language arrived. Before that, we existed in a domain of raw unity. Now, words shape our reality. For the San, that is not mere metaphor but a lived phenomenon. They see the foot-stomping circle as a place where that primal unity can be partially reclaimed, but it still hinges on the right incantations. The synergy of chant, motion, and carefully arranged clicks is the route to bridging the gap.

Those who have studied these tongues academically might marvel at the phonetic system, enumerating alveolar, lateral, palatal, labial, and retroflex clicks. But from a spiritual vantage, that complexity is not just intellectual. It is a sign that the language has developed extraordinary nuance to express countless variations of meaning. In daily conversation, those clicks become routine. However, the moment a sacred word is invoked or an archaic chant is begun, everyone senses the link to a deeper plane. Children learn them by hearing, repeating, occasionally being corrected if they insert the wrong click at the wrong moment. Over time, their entire worldview gains shape: they can name the ancestors, they can name intangible energies, they can name subtle variations of the foot-stomping ceremony or the difference between a communal event and a home-based healing session. Each distinction lies in the vocabulary.

One detail that always intrigued me is the presence of metaphorical statements in everyday talk. If a healer says, "The lion inside you is hungry," that might be literal or figurative. Linguistically, the phrase might incorporate click sounds that evoke an actual lion's growl or footsteps, giving it a potent effect on the listener. Another scenario might involve saying, "Your water has gone dry," to indicate someone has lost vitality or luck. The blending of physical resource references with intangible states is typical. A single word can pivot from describing the dryness of a waterhole to diagnosing the emptiness in a person's spirit. That elasticity in meaning is no accident. It arises because the culture does not see nature and spirit as separate compartments. Indeed, the lexicon reflects that merged perspective.

 Tying language to music is the final note that sparks my admiration. Traditional foot-stomping circles rely heavily on repeated chant lines, some of which have a recognized lexical meaning, while others are ancient sequences of clicks and tones passed down as part of the "songs from God." A Giraffe Song might revolve around the movement or essence of that tall creature, but also hold the capacity to quicken n/um in the participants. Contemporary participants say that singing these lines connects them to a lineage of ancestors who originally discovered them. If that is so, then the language is not just shaped by immediate social usage but by a generational chain of spiritual experiences. Those who chant them sense the presence of all who came before, infusing the moment with a resonance that transcends immediate time. And while certain phrases might remain incomprehensible to an outsider, the community knows that those syllables are part of a broader tapestry of intangible communications.

When I reflect on the fragility of these languages in the modern era—some with only a handful of fluent elders—I feel a pang of concern for the potential loss of intangible knowledge. The outward lexical forms are more than historical artifacts. They are keys that open ancient storerooms of meaning, keys that can vanish if not spoken regularly. Yet at the same time, the durability these tongues have exhibited across centuries is astounding. Without writing or official backing, they have traveled through countless generations. This success arises from an environment where learning by ear was mandatory, and where spiritual significance attached to every phrase. Indeed, the foot-stomping practice itself, with its repetitive calls, has served as a method of reinforcing memory. The same repeated lines that help ignite n/um also drill crucial words into young minds. In that sense, the ceremonies are not just healing tools but also cultural schools.

In sum, these click-filled tongues remain guardians of a spiritual perspective that sees the world as deeply layered. Each expression, each specialized term, each melodic refrain, each metaphor, each click itself is a path to intangible realms. Whether describing the intense inner flame called n/um, the half-death state known as !kia, or the haunted domain of gauwasi (spirits), the words carry an uncanny vitality. They keep an oral encyclopedia alive in a community that relies on no written documents, instead trusting in the power of repeated telling and chanting. Perhaps that is one reason the foot-stomping events can be so electrifying: they do not rely on an external text or a liturgy pinned to a page. The text resides in the memory of the people, and the ceremony mobilizes it through chanting, swaying, and communal synergy.

I remember one final anecdote. A mother taught her daughter a short melodic line for summoning "small blessings." She explained that this line had to be sung in the early morning while facing east, paired with a gentle series of claps. The daughter struggled to master the timing of the clicks embedded in the tune. But once she succeeded, her mother assured her that she now had the means to call upon daily fortune. Outside observers might see it as a superstition, but for them, it was an act of passing down an ancient incantation that hinged on correct phonetics. Even that small example illustrates the function of language as a spiritual bridge for personal well-being. Step by step, mothers pass it on to daughters, uncles pass it on to nephews, and so forth. The result is a chain that preserves intangible wisdom.

Whenever I hear a snippet of Ju/'hoan or !Xũ in recordings, I am struck again by how profoundly it resonates with the environment, the personal identity of the speaker, and the threads of myth that define their cosmos. These are not tongues to be studied in isolation from the spiritual practices. They are fully embedded in them. The use of metaphor, onomatopoeia, specialized vocabulary, archaic chant lines, and the consistent references to intangible forces all speak to a worldview in which language and spirituality are braided together. If either is lost, the other inevitably weakens.

Perhaps that is why so many San elders emphasize the importance of teaching children the old songs and stories from an early age. They see it as more than a cultural flourish. It is their legacy, their inheritance from those who came before, and it is the conduit to intangible resources that have helped them navigate an arid, challenging environment for countless generations. N/um is ignited in the foot-stomping circle, but the instructions for reaching that ignition are all locked within the mother tongue. A chant might call forth ancestors, or it might mimic the rustle of an animal in the bush, or it might do both. That layering underscores the majesty and complexity of these tongues, which have guided entire communities through hardship and triumph.

So the next time you hear about click consonants, do not imagine it as a quaint linguistic oddity or a mere footnote in some anthropological record. Instead, envision a living tapestry of meaning: men and women chanting those clicks under starry skies, calling on Eland potency, bridging the gap between the living and the departed, protecting children from harm, blessing new hunts. Each click is a spark in the night, fueling an oral tradition that has flourished across the deserts, shaped moral codes, safeguarded communal identity, and connected these people to their ancestors in ways that outsiders can only partially grasp. And that, in my eyes, is the real heart of what these languages hold. The synergy of sound, memory, metaphor, and faith is woven into every subtle nuance, ensuring that the intangible heritage of the San moves through time by way of the word, the chant, and the unstoppable perseverance of those who carry it forward, one breath at a time.

Shamanic Wisdom Through Time

I can never forget the first time I pressed my palm against an ancient rock face in the Drakensberg Mountains and gazed upon those ochre outlines of half-human, half-animal figures. People told me they were possibly 20,000 years old or more, crafted by the distant ancestors of the San, who left behind these mysterious portrayals of dancing shapes, elongated limbs, and swirling patterns that still hint at the supernatural realm. It struck me like a vision across time: that a people dwelling in the so-called Stone Age could have created such profound, layered images. In those weathered contours, we see hints of bent dancers, seemingly bleeding at the nose, locked in the ecstatic postures that modern observers recognize from contemporary trance ceremonies. Even geometric shapes like spirals, dots, and zigzags, once shrugged off as decorative flourishes, are now interpreted by scholars like J. David Lewis-Williams as entoptic phenomena—fleeting visuals encountered in the altered states of consciousness. It's astonishing to realize these rock walls can be read as galleries of shamanic exploration. Therianthropes—beings that merge human form with the heads or hooves or horns of animals—appear frequently, suggesting the moment a shaman in trance might become, in spirit, an Eland or a rain-beast. Right alongside that we see Eland motifs, with the giant antelope towering large and majestic, much as it does in modern San ceremonies. That recurring Eland presence in the art underscores the old stories describing it as a reservoir of power, the very creature that might embody healing, potency, and a direct link to the intangible. And so, from Tsodilo Hills in Botswana to the Brandberg in Namibia, from the Drakensberg to lesser-known sites scattered across the subcontinent, we find these prehistoric time capsules of a worldview that invests dance and vision with cosmic significance.

The archaeologists, of course, uncover stone implements, arrow points, and the debris of everyday life in these caves and shelters, but I find the rock images more captivating than any potsherd. It seems that long before anything akin to a formal written language, the ancestors were depicting the realm of the spirit—shamans ascending to the sky or drawing power from the Eland's essence, dancers contorting or floating. Here we have a testament that the "shamanic secret" of the San, the capacity to induce trance and commune with hidden energies, is no recent invention. Rather, it is an inheritance from humanity's earliest spiritual explorations, persisting through unimaginable stretches of time. To stand there in that quiet space, feeling the hush of the ancient stone, is to connect with a dimension of continuity that has spanned millennia.

    Still, the story is not solely one of timeless heritage but also one of upheaval and adaptation. Over many centuries, the San encountered waves of newcomers into southern Africa. Bantu-speaking farmers and pastoralists spread southward some 1,500 or more years ago, gradually supplanting or assimilating certain groups. Then, much later, came European settlers, who seized land, fenced it, and introduced new economies. The San, famed for their nimble hunter-gatherer ways, saw their territories carved up. Some tried to keep living as they had, but many were forced into labor or cast onto marginal lands. During these disruptions, entire groups vanished or blended into larger communities. Nonetheless, the resilient core of San spirituality persisted, especially in remote pockets such as the Kalahari Desert. From the 1950s onward, anthropologists like Lorna and John Marshall, Elizabeth Marshall Thomas, and Richard Lee stumbled upon living bands who still performed trance dances four or more times a month. In these out-of-the-way corners, the essence of their old worldview was intact, even if aspects of material life had shifted.

Observers noted that while the healing rituals endured, the trappings changed. Instead of the pristine cocoon rattles once used, some dancers tied together tin cans or bits of modern rubbish to mimic the rattle effect. Where once a man might have worn an Eland tail as a spiritual talisman, maybe now he adopted a scrap of cloth or a beaded ornament to embody the same power. In some communities, Christianity seeped into these ceremonies, resulting in a syncretic practice. A shaman might invoke the "Great God" the same way older traditions did, but then interpret certain trance images in a Christian framework. I once heard a man say that Jesus and Kaggen (Mantis) were aspects of the same luminous force. Another group refused such blending, determined to maintain the older references unaltered. Observing that range of responses made it clear that there is no single monolithic reaction to outside influence. The Kalahari, broad as it is, fosters many distinct pockets of culture, each with its own path of resilience.

Not all changes arose from oppression or forced assimilation. Some San communities recognized that tourism could offer a lifeline. They began performing dances for visitors, sometimes in curated events at lodges or cultural festivals. The Kuru Dance Festival in Botswana, for instance, is renowned for featuring San healing dances in a public, intercultural showcase. Critics worry that turning these sacred ceremonies into spectacles risks trivializing or commodifying them, yet some local participants argue that it also provides a platform for younger generations to learn the old steps, songs, and rituals in a celebratory context. I remember hearing a woman say, "We would rather show them how we dance than let it fade in secret." That statement, though controversial, revealed a pragmatism about preserving tradition by adapting to new economic realities.

Of course, the biggest challenge arises from land dispossession. Many San now live in settlements far from their ancestral n!ore, reliant on meager government rations or menial jobs. One elder described how the fences and cattle ranches had dried out the land, draining it of wild game, waterholes, and the intangible presence that used to support communal ceremonies. If families cannot gather in the old places, the impetus to hold large-scale trance dances might wane. Alcohol abuse is another lamentable byproduct of forced sedentarization. When people feel cut off from their heritage, jobless, or alienated, destructive coping mechanisms can seep in. These conditions weaken the communal structure that sustained trance healing. I recall one older man recalling with sorrow how they used to hold a dance every couple of weeks in his youth, but now, in the settlement, the younger men prefer to drink at a local shebeen or watch television if they can. The impetus to dance fades unless specifically revived by an elder.

Despite all this, I have witnessed stirring examples of cultural revival. Some San-led organizations partner with NGOs to reclaim land rights or to establish heritage projects. They might record elders' stories, preserve the songs, or run language workshops for children. Others coordinate with communities in D'Kar, Nyae Nyae, or scattered enclaves in Angola and South Africa, encouraging them to preserve the old ceremonies. People like Richard Katz and Megan Biesele have pointed out that the dance is not just spiritual. It carries psychosocial benefits that help a group maintain solidarity and positivity amid outside pressures. Singing, dancing, and "boiling" n/um together fosters emotional catharsis and a sense of mutual support. If you lose that, you lose more than a religion: you lose a form of communal therapy that has anchored them for centuries.

I have spoken to younger San who say they want the best of both worlds: they appreciate certain aspects of modern schooling, maybe want to find work in nearby towns, but also feel an urge to keep the foot-stomping tradition alive. They say it's part of who they are, a link to the grandparents, and an expression of identity that can't be replaced by any church service or government program. One can sense their ambivalence: do they remain in the settlement, try to eke out a living, or do they fight to return to the desert, recapturing the band-based foraging life that their ancestors knew? In many places, the question is moot because the land is gone or privatized.

But a handful of projects, sometimes under the banner of "cultural survival" or "land restitution," strive to give communities partial control of their historical grounds again, or at least some agency in how they represent their traditions to the outside world.

The reality is that the total number of San is drastically lower than in pre-colonial times. Some scholars estimate only a fraction remain who speak the older tongues fluently. Others have integrated into mainstream Bantu groups or towns and seldom recall the old ceremonies. This decline, painful though it is, does not erase the fact that certain enclaves hold fast. By documenting their songs, equipping them with resources, or celebrating their events in a dignified manner, these enclaves can remain living strongholds of a tradition that has endured for untold centuries. I recall meeting a Ju/'hoan elder in Namibia who expressed fierce pride that they continued to dance. "We do it for ourselves," he said. "We do it for the ones who came before and the children who are here now. Even if the rest of the world forgets us, we remember." That quiet resolve has allowed the tradition to traverse waves of adversity.

In an increasingly interconnected world, a new issue arises: appropriation. There is a segment of New Age or neo-shamanic circles that eagerly adopt bits and pieces of indigenous practice to create their own spiritual retreats and workshops. Some invite participants to "experience an authentic Bushman trance dance" far away from Africa, taught by an instructor who might have visited the Kalahari once or read a few anthropological texts. They promise spiritual enlightenment for a fee, but rarely do they credit or compensate the communities from which these methods are borrowed. This can flatten the cultural nuance of the practice, turning it into a homogenized brand of exoticism. San elders and activists have voiced frustration that such a phenomenon robs them of their intellectual and spiritual property while trivializing the deeper significance of the foot-stomping circle. They want to stress that a dance that emerged from centuries of living close to the land, from communal foraging, from a nuanced language of clicks and chants, cannot be fully replicated in a weekend workshop. It might offer a taste of the experience, but lacking the entire matrix of relationships, land, language, and shared meaning, it risks becoming a shallow mimicry. Some practitioners in the West, however well-intentioned, might not realize the historical traumas or land dispossession behind the tradition they are borrowing.

Hence the emphasis: if outsiders wish to learn from the San, permission, context, and reciprocity matter deeply. One local example is the Cultural Survival program that helps bring actual San storytellers and healers abroad to lead sessions or workshops, so the tradition is explained by those who live it daily, and any profits can return to sustain the community. This approach tries to ensure that the original holders of the knowledge guide how it is presented. Similarly, anthropologists who share research with the public often highlight that the iconic Eland in rock art is not an alien or a mere drug-induced hallucination but a significant religious symbol. The same caution extends to the entire notion of calling them "primitive." That label has overshadowed the sophisticated spirituality and social resilience found among the San. They never needed advanced architecture to develop a rich, nuanced worldview that has enthralled anthropologists for generations.

Looking back, one sees that the earliest scientific explorations of the 19th century sometimes treated San stories and images as oddities, even ridiculing them. Gradually, recognition grew that these stories hold deep insight into the human condition. Rock art studies, for instance, once dismissed the paintings as "hunting magic," but now we realize many are explicitly linked to the trance experience. The cultural lens shifted from seeing them as curiosities to seeing them as a refined system of symbolic representation. That shift in academic approach parallels the broader shift in how the San are perceived: from "savages" to masters of an ancient knowledge system. Yet, that reappraisal alone does not shield them from the real issues of poverty, land dispossession, and paternalistic policies. The hope is that shining a respectful light on their traditions, and supporting tangible improvements in their living conditions, can help preserve not only the old ways but also the dignity of the communities themselves.

It's easy for me to stand in awe of those miraculous rock paintings or the mesmerizing trance dance. But for the San, it's not about wowing tourists or fulfilling anthropological theories: it's about survival, identity, healing, and moral guidance. In that sense, the foot-stomping ceremony is a microcosm of their entire philosophy: it's communal, physically demanding, oriented around intangible energies, requiring concentration and memory, passing from elders to youth. This single activity weaves together so many threads— mythic narratives of the Eland or Kaggen, the harnessing of n/um, the forging of social cohesion, the language of subtle clicks and chants. And though changes have come (in the form of new materials or partial Christian influences), the essence is still there. Indeed, the same potent dance that was etched onto rock walls thousands of years ago continues in dusty settlement squares, in special festival venues, or in hidden pockets of bushland where families gather in the hush of night.

One cannot ignore the heartbreak of a diminished population, or the tragedies of land usurpation, diseases, and the exploitation that accompanied colonial expansions. Yet the counterpoint is the resilience of the San. They have found ways to adapt: using tin-can rattles, offering truncated performances for tourists to generate income, or layering Christian names onto the old spirit references. They keep dancing, singing, and telling stories, thus refusing to vanish into footnotes. I see that as a testament to the strength of their belief in the intangible as well as the practicality of their approach. The anthropologists of the mid-20th century were astounded to see how effectively the trance dance helped them handle stress and conflict. The same dance might keep sustaining them as they navigate the transformations of the 21st century. People like Katz and Biesele argue that such communal healing is a cornerstone that may well ensure cultural continuity, even as the world around them moves at breakneck speed.

If the outside world supports them through respectful partnerships—grants for language revitalization, recognition of land claims, endorsements of their intangible heritage, and ethical forms of cultural exchange—then the path forward can remain open. If, on the contrary, these traditions are lifted wholesale as an exotic commodity and sold without proper context, it only deepens the sense of injustice. Thus, the conversation around "preservation versus appropriation" is not theoretical: it directly impacts whether future generations of San can define themselves, continue speaking their languages, and approach the sacred n/um dance in the old way. The line between genuine cross-cultural respect and exploitation can be fine, but it is absolutely crucial to walk it with honesty.

    Observing from a bigger vantage, I see that the rock art stands as a silent witness to all these shifts. Those paintings remain in caves or on sheltered cliffs, immune to immediate human meddling except for the threat of vandalism or erosion. They speak of a time when entire populations engaged in trance-based ritual as a central pillar of life, melding daily survival with cosmic engagement. Today's smaller, marginalized groups, with battered economies, still hold those same keys—

but must fight for the space to use them. Even so, they show no sign of giving up. NGOs and local associations keep pushing for improvements, while anthropologists and cultural activists lend support in documenting stories, encouraging language classes, and raising awareness about the deeper significance of the foot-stomping tradition. Every year, new volunteers arrive, hoping to record testimonies from the oldest living shamans, or to help set up local exhibitions of rock art images. In the most optimistic scenarios, young San discover a spark of pride in these efforts and decide to learn the old ways, seeing them as both an inheritance and a source of empowerment.

Throughout it all, the Eland remains. So does the memory of an intangible dimension that can be reached by human hearts and bodies in motion, accompanied by the layering of song. Anyone witnessing a live healing dance would sense that continuity linking the present generation to those who painted caves 10,000 or 20,000 years ago. In the hush of a desert night, with dust swirling up under stamping feet, and voices rising in high-pitched calls, you catch a glimpse of that primal connection.

The trembling dancer pulls out sickness, flings it away, just as a rock painting once showed a figure in mid-transformation. The final hush at dawn is the same hush that has fallen over countless dawns in the deep past, bridging any chronological chasm with living breath.

Yes, the 21st century puts new demands on the old heritage, but it also brings new audiences. Some travelers arrive with genuine respect, determined to learn about the complexities of this tradition from the people themselves, not from a superficial brochure. Meanwhile, technology allows for digital archiving of stories and songs, giving them a fresh lease on life. One can imagine future community members, decades from now, revisiting video recordings of a grandmother's healing dance and gleaning from it the impetus to reclaim that knowledge. So, ironically, the same modernity that threatens their old lifestyle might also become an avenue for preserving the intangible. Of course, the interplay is delicate, and not all solutions are foolproof. But there is hope in the synergy between local determination and carefully managed outside assistance.

And so, to anyone enthralled by the timeless images of half-human beings or the mesmerizing swirl of dancing figures on the rocks, I urge you to remember that this is not just ancient art. It is an ongoing story, a legacy carried by real communities who still sing, dance, and face daily challenges. Their worldview, their language, their reverence for Eland, their trust in n/um, and the foot-stomping ceremony itself comprise an unbroken chain that ties together the prehistoric and the modern. That is a remarkable feat of cultural endurance, one that can still captivate and instruct us about how to inhabit the Earth with heart, body, and spirit engaged as one. If we approach it with humility, acknowledging that it is first and foremost the San's inheritance, then perhaps we might find our own human perspective enriched in the process. They have always lived with the idea that humans flourish best when in rhythmic conversation with the land and its hidden powers, and that is a lesson that resonates far beyond the bounds of the Kalahari. In the end, the foot-stomping circle stands as a universal testament to collective healing and spiritual quest

—a testament that has survived from the ancient rock shelters to our present day, and that may well guide the next century if we honor the people whose ancestors first shaped it.

Ancient Astronaut Theories and the San

I remember first coming across an "ancient astronauts" proposal in a rather tattered pamphlet at a roadside curio stall, just on the outskirts of Ghanzi, Botswana. Its lurid illustrations suggested that the strange figures in San rock art were indeed beings from outer space, wearing helmets and brandishing futuristic tools. My eyes widened a bit, because I was more accustomed to reading the standard anthropological accounts linking these images to shamanic trance experiences, not cosmic visitors. But it was fascinating to see how readily some people latch onto the notion that what looks alien to them must literally be aliens. And the San's mesmerizing cosmos, with star-lore and open skies, certainly invites speculation in popular culture.

A single short paragraph can barely scratch the surface of these theories, so let me dive deeper. The "ancient astronauts" hypothesis, at its core, argues that many of the myths, megalithic structures, or unusual artifacts from ancient human civilizations are best explained by contact with extraterrestrials. While mainstream archaeology and anthropology see them as products of local cultural development, fringe theorists maintain that advanced cosmic visitors left behind footprints. For the San, the conversation typically revolves around a handful of painted images that might look to casual observers like "spacecraft," "portals," or "alien heads." Add to that the fact that the San talk about star people, or speak of journeys into the sky during trance, and you have the recipe for an internet-fueled swirl of speculation.

But let's talk about the actual star motifs in San myth. These are a people who live under some of the world's clearest night skies, in landscapes unlit by city glare, meaning the heavens appear in all their blazing glory. The San have always needed to navigate across wide, arid territories, and so their keen observation of seasonal changes, the position of the moon, and the rising constellations should not be surprising. They speak of the sun, moon, and stars as if these celestial bodies are personal entities or manifestations of spiritual forces. A tale might describe the sun as a once-lazy man's glowing head that had to be thrown into the sky for the benefit of all, or the moon as a piece of |Kaggen's shoe. Typically, the star cluster called Orion's Belt might be named a line of tortoises or even three pigs, signifying the cosmic drama that unfolds nightly in that region of sky. It's a thoroughly imaginative approach, but it doesn't require outside help from space travelers to explain. The thirst for cosmic wonder has always lived in the human mind.

People who see UFOs in these paintings tend to ignore the broader ritual context.

Another aspect fueling speculation is the presence of bizarre shapes in some rock art, particularly in places like Zimbabwe's Matobo Hills, where swirling ovals and circles appear. In photographs, they can look eerily reminiscent of portals or energy fields as might be depicted in science fiction. One can indeed muse that these shapes might represent stargates or cosmic wormholes. But if you spend much time with San elders or anthropologists who have studied these images, you'll find consistent interpretations pointing to spiritual doorways relevant to trance states. In such states, the boundary between the visible and invisible dissolves. Shamans speak of traveling across thresholds into other realms, encountering ancestors or powerful animals. So, from a purely cultural viewpoint, these oval shapes fit better with the concept of a trance-induced spirit passage rather than futuristic technology. In many cases, the "portals" align with natural cracks or depressions in the rock wall. Ancient San painters apparently incorporated these natural features into their symbolic imagery—maybe a crack in the rock was the perfect place to show a spirit or a magical opening.

Of course, none of this stops certain enthusiasts from proclaiming that these cracks and shapes must be the residue of alien landings. They point to big-eyed figures, or images that appear to have antennae, as "proof" that the local artists witnessed space suits. But in most contexts, these forms are understood to be stylized depictions of shamans transforming or adopting insect traits, tying in with the Mantis deity figure or with animal spirits. The "antennae" might be the mantis's forelegs drawn upright on a shaman's head, or some representation of intangible energy streaming from the dancer's crown. Across many samples of southern African rock art, you see repeated patterns of lines emanating from the head or limbs of painted figures, usually explained by experts as a visual code for the supernatural potency that radiates from a trance specialist.

It's curious how outsiders sometimes need to project outer space into ancient pictures, when the reality is that the ancient artists were describing an inner space: a realm accessed by rhythm, dance, and mind-altering states that require no advanced technology. In parallel, people who champion "ancient aliens" as the source of these abilities often overlook the extraordinary capacity for observation and myth-making that humans have always possessed. The same innovative leaps that let the San navigate deserts by starlight or interpret the phases of the moon might seem magical to someone unfamiliar with how nuanced oral knowledge can be. If we consider that the San's ancestors studied the sky nightly for thousands of years, it's only natural they would develop mythic connections to constellations, name them in creative ways, and integrate these concepts into their spiritual worldview. The wonder is that modern folks find that so improbable, they'd rather chalk it up to external cosmic tutors.

  I recall meeting a group of travelers who had visited the Matobo Hills and came away convinced they'd seen a UFO depiction. They told me the swirling lines around a floating shape proved that ancient Africans once encountered star visitors. But when I pressed them on the broader scene—did it also show animals, dancers, or contextual features?—they admitted that yes, there were also stylized human figures, possibly in some kind of ceremony. In other words, the alleged "craft" was part of a shamanic tableau. They still clung to the idea that it might be an alien craft intruding upon that ceremony, but I walked away thinking how differently those paintings appear if one has read about entoptic patterns and the typical geometry of trance visuals. Nonetheless, I realize that the human imagination is vast, and some prefer a cosmic storyline.

The anthropologist David Lewis-Williams famously wrote about how the rock art's "other-worldly" dimension actually reflects the vantage of a person in an altered state, seeing vivid hallucinations that are then shaped by cultural metaphors. Those entoptic forms—dots, grids, spirals—are common cross-culturally in shamanic or visionary art. The presence of big eyes, elongated bodies, or partial transformations doesn't require the presence of aliens. If anything, it underscores the widespread phenomenon of the mind's capacity to conjure up kaleidoscopes of shapes when it crosses a certain threshold of consciousness. The entire "portal to another dimension" motif can be accepted as real in a spiritual sense, a trance reality, rather than a literal portal to another planet. The San themselves talk about traveling to the sky, or to an underworld, or to the domain of the gods, all within the medicine dance context. But they do not attribute these feats to advanced extraterrestrials. Instead, they point to n/um, the internal boiling energy that lets them scale intangible threads. Why complicate it with UFOs?

One reason the ancient astronaut idea intrigues people is that humans across different continents share certain mythic motifs, like powerful beings descending from the sky, or stories of floods, or tales about primeval visitors who taught essential skills. Some authors highlight parallels between a San story of a bee ferrying Mantis across a flooded world and the many global flood myths. They say perhaps it's proof of a real event or some universal memory of alien saviors. But flood myths are nearly universal for simpler reasons—floods are a widespread phenomenon, and water is a critical resource. They serve as potent symbols of destruction and rebirth, so it is no surprise that distinct cultures imagine cosmic floods. Meanwhile, the details—like a bee carrying Mantis—are more readily explained by local symbolic logic: the bee is crucial in the desert for honey, pollination, water detection, so it stands to reason it would appear in a heroic role. The leap to aliens is unnecessary.

Furthermore, the San historically didn't construct large stone edifices or elaborate megastructures that might suggest improbable engineering feats. Ancient astronaut theories often revolve around puzzling architectural wonders—Egypt's pyramids, Mesoamerican temples, or the Nazca lines in Peru. The San's rock art, by comparison, is not about building monumental sites but about painting ephemeral images on natural rock surfaces. The artistry can be advanced in a symbolic sense, but it doesn't rely on the kind of large-scale geometry that sets alarm bells ringing in the heads of fringe theorists. So, ironically, the San usually occupy only a marginal place in the "ancient aliens" conversation. Occasionally, they appear in passing references to rock art that might depict "otherworldly figures," or in claims that their star-lore references some esoteric cosmic knowledge. But those who have studied the tradition see it as a wholly earthbound spiritual system, albeit one that poetically interprets the heavens.

Now, let's consider the question of advanced astronomical knowledge. Did the San precisely measure planetary orbits or note star cycles like Sirius's helical rising? There is little direct evidence for that. They certainly recognized seasonal changes keyed to constellations, the onset of the rainy or dry season, or hunting migrations. But it was a practical knowledge integrated with mythic perspectives, not the formal astronomy that might involve carefully recorded observational data or stone alignments. Some stories revolve around individuals climbing to the sky and becoming stars, or tossing objects that transform into clusters. One might point to that and say, "Look, they recognized that a cluster was once a single entity." But really, that's more an example of mythic creativity. The line between literal star science and narrative is fluid in this culture. The fact that an early human or an insect soared up to become a star cluster is less about measuring cosmic distances and more about forging spiritual kinship with the night sky. People rely on these mythic narratives to anchor their sense of place in the cosmos, not to calculate eclipses with scientific precision.

Yet, that mythic approach is no less sophisticated in its own domain. Many ancient societies had star-lore of this sort, weaving it into the moral and ritual tapestry of daily life. The "ancient aliens" perspective often mistakes sophisticated conceptual or symbolic systems for a sign of advanced exogenous technology. But humans are perfectly capable of brilliance without help from the Pleiades or Zeta Reticuli. The San may talk about times when earth and sky were so close they touched, or when animals and people lived above. That is a poetic expression of the fluid boundaries they experience in trance, the sense that one can slip between earthly and heavenly planes. It emerges from repeated communal ceremonies, from shared dreams, from thousands of years of living in synergy with nature's rhythms. If an alien landed, one wonders if the San might have painted it outright as some bizarre beast. But we see no clear sign of that. Instead, we see Eland, we see mantis-humans, we see geometric expansions of a dancer's form. It's a spiritually charged interior world, not an alien invasion.

I once had a whimsical conversation with a local elder about whether Mantis might be an alien from beyond Earth, given his shape-shifting powers. She laughed mightily and said Mantis is part of everything, here. She indicated that if Mantis had come from somewhere else, it must have been "the spirit place," not from a different planet. Indeed, that suggests that for them, the real question is bridging the spiritual and the material, rather than bridging Earth and outer space. The starlore in many stories describes the dead rising to become lights in the sky, or how certain constellations represent animals that parted ways with humankind. These are not at all reminiscent of visiting starships or cosmic teachers. Instead, they proclaim the cosmic integration of life and death, reminding the living that ancestors watch overhead. In that sense, the "star people" for the San are more precisely the "ancestral watchers," not a race of technologically advanced aliens. If anything, the mythic references to going skyward highlight the significance of shamanic flight. But that's an inner flight, ignited by n/um and trance, rather than rocket science.

We must also recall that the entire phenomenon of labeling the San "primitive" or "Stone Age relics" is often layered with colonial stereotypes. So, people might be predisposed to think, "Surely these folks couldn't come up with these ideas on their own—they must have had help." The same condescending impulse once led people to assume that any great African achievement, from monumental architecture to iron smelting, must have come from outside influences. That paternalistic approach has been debunked, but it resurfaces in new guises when alternative theorists try to argue that "primitive bushmen" depict aliens. Meanwhile, many members of the San communities themselves wonder why the outside world can't just accept that their ancestors had spiritual depth and imaginative power. Indeed, even in other parts of Africa, like the Dogon people of Mali, there have been controversies claiming they had advanced knowledge of Sirius B's existence, leading to speculations about alien revelation. Later scholarship found the story more complicated and possibly shaped by outside informants. Something similar could happen with the San if people impose an "alien visitation" narrative onto them. But as of now, there is no strong evidence that the San possessed or claimed a scientific insight that would require ET tutoring.

Those who do cling to the ancient astronaut idea for the San sometimes rely on tangential references. For instance, they might mention that the world was flooded and Mantis was saved by a bee. They then compare this to Sumerian or Mesoamerican floods, hoping to find a link to a single ancient cataclysm triggered by aliens. But each region's flood myths typically revolve around moral or ecological lessons, not revelations from the stars. The bee in the San story is obviously central to desert survival, not a coded reference to some insectoid alien race. Another claim might revolve around a magic comb flung into the sky to become the Pleiades, which is also a widespread motif in global star lore: objects turning into celestial bodies. But it is a sign of creative storytelling, not an advanced orbital mapping project. All these data points are better explained by an imaginative, mythopoetic worldview than by literal cosmic visitors with high-tech gear.

To be fair, there is a sense in which the San rock art can look "outer worldly," especially if you come from a Western background where typical art focuses on literal scenes or purely decorative patterns. The half-human, half-antelope silhouettes, the swirling lines around them, the halos or arcs that circle a figure's head—these can produce an uncanny vibe. Then add the majestic emptiness of those rock shelters, the desert hush, and the feeling that you've stepped back in time 20,000 years. It's easy to see how the mind might leap to cosmic fantasies. But the truth is that these paintings revolve around the logic of trance journeys, the transformation of the self into an animal or spirit form, the intangible geometry of entoptic visions. Anthropologists call it "shamanic flight," not "flight in a spaceship."

Some travelers ask, "Couldn't both be true—maybe the shamans encountered aliens in trance?" Ultimately, we can't rule out any imaginative possibility in the absolute sense, but there is no direct testimony from the San themselves about meeting advanced beings from other planets or seeing mechanical craft. Their stories revolve around Kaggen (the Mantis) or Eland potency or star ancestors, all of which remain anchored in a local environment shaped by desert survival, communal dancing, and a fluid sense of the spiritual domain. When pressed on "ancient alien" possibilities, many elders show mild amusement or confusion. They know their ancestors were wise and imaginative, so they see no reason to credit star visitors for that wisdom. If anything, the impetus to find aliens can overshadow the more interesting question of how humans invented shamanism and cosmic mythology in the first place.

Indeed, one line of research suggests that shamanic ritual might date back 100,000 years or more, preceding the diaspora of

Homo sapiens out of Africa. That would make the San (among the most genetically ancient populations) key living bearers of primal shamanic practices. The mesmerizing parallels between San rock art and certain European Upper Paleolithic cave art might reflect a shared deep heritage of altered-state representation. Some older theories claimed that people around the world share these "mysterious" spiritual impulses because we had a single archaic experience of "aliens." But it's far more plausible that these experiences of trance and the illusions of cosmic or spiritual travel are intrinsic to human consciousness, not triggered externally by space visitors. The same universal neuropsychological processes that produce entoptic patterns in one region can yield them in another. That is a simpler, more elegant explanation than postulating an interplanetary expedition dropping off the secrets of the universe in scattered spots around Earth.

Recent discoveries in southern Africa keep expanding our awareness of how deeply the San engaged with their environment and how they may have integrated knowledge of local fauna, plants, and even fossils. If, for example, they saw unusual fossils or bones in a dry creek bed, they might weave them into myths about monstrous creatures from earlier epochs. That readiness to incorporate ancient remains into spiritual narratives underscores their capacity for imagination and inquiry. But again, none of it requires an alien origin. Quite the contrary, it reveals a people curious about their own land's deep past, open to blending natural history with visionary states to produce a tapestry of meaning. Should we find faint paintings of bizarre reptilian forms, it might reflect a mythic story about monstrous beasts or an attempt to depict discovered bones. The leap to aliens is purely an overlay from a modern worldview hungry for cosmic drama.

So, it seems that for every alleged "alien" element in San tradition, there's a straightforward cultural or spiritual explanation. That does not make it any less enchanting. Their star-lore, their paintings, their sense of climbing invisible threads to the sky, remain profoundly stirring. If someone loves the idea of cosmic wonder, they can still relish the fact that the San approach is already cosmic in its own symbolic sense, bridging mortality and infinity through trance. You don't need literal UFOs to experience that sense of cosmic awe. Indeed, the real power of the San tradition might lie in how it encourages us to look inward—toward the capacities of human consciousness and the creative depths of mythmaking. If you stare at a painting in a hidden rock shelter and see swirling lines that evoke the entire universe, that's the hallmark of the human mind at its most visionary, not necessarily a message from the Pleiades.

Once, I stood at the edge of a campsite near Tsodilo Hills, late at night, scanning the pitch-black sky spangled with countless stars. A local friend told me a story about how her grandmother used to say that each star is a person who has passed on but still shines with guidance for the living. She never mentioned aliens, but she did mention that sometimes, in dream or trance, you can visit them up there, speak with them, and ask for wisdom. That perspective is cosmic in the truest sense: bridging life and death, matter and spirit, starglow and human emotion. If someone from a "ancient astronauts" vantage hears that, they might exclaim, "Ah, star beings, so it's about aliens." But they would be missing the emotional and communal essence: it's about ancestors. It's about memory, continuity, and the luminous promise that each life, after departing, becomes a light in the night. There's nothing about advanced propulsion or foreign star systems. It's purely an earth-centric spirituality that acknowledges the night sky as part of one's extended family.

In the end, we can appreciate that the "ancient astronaut" crowd occasionally stumbles across fascinating rock art or intriguing star-lore but then leaps to solutions that sidestep the cultural matrix. Meanwhile, mainstream anthropology reaffirms that these images and stories are best understood as elements of shamanic artistry, animistic cosmology, and a symbolic approach to the heavens that humans have practiced since time immemorial. The San, for their part, continue to dance, sing, and honor the starry vault without needing to claim any off-world authorship. And for me, that's more than enough to keep the sense of wonder alive. Their intangible knowledge, bridging body, spirit, earth, and sky, is so deep and multifaceted that it already stands among humanity's greatest treasures. Adding "aliens" to the mix might be fun for a late-night TV show, but it pales next to the living reality of the foot-stomping ceremony and the Eland-laden rock paintings that speak to internal universes.

If you ever find yourself in the Matobo Hills or near any of those desert shelters, you might find a scrawl that, in a photograph, looks bizarrely futuristic. In person, though, you'll probably see it integrated with a scene of stylized dancers or animals. You'll sense the hush of that place, the faint echoes of long-ago chants, the imprint of thousands of footsteps passing through. The "mystery," in that moment, reveals itself as something far richer than extraterrestrial speculation: it's about the capacity of human beings to interpret reality at multiple levels, weaving physical survival with spiritual flights. No saucer required. That's the real gift that the San rock art and their star-lore convey to the modern world. And if you truly want to honor their genius, let it inspire you to look inward, to see how we all share that primal spark of imagination, that potential to recast the everyday sky into a tapestry of meaning, rather than chasing ephemeral illusions of aliens who probably never set foot in the Kalahari.

Ritual Reconstruction

Just as the Kalahari resonates with the quiet patter of feet and the echo of voices raised in song, so too can we create a space in which the intangible dimension of energy—n/um—unfolds. In the paragraphs that follow, you'll find a proposed structure: from setting the stage at sunset to the final hush that greets the dawn. Let these words serve as a respectful outline only. Remember that the true depth arises from living knowledge held by the San people themselves, who have danced beneath starlit skies for thousands of years.

INTRODUCTORY THOUGHTS AND ETHICAL CONTEXT

Imagine stepping onto the sands at twilight, feeling the day's heat fade into a gentle breeze as the sun surrenders to a velvet sky. Perhaps you stand at the edge of a small clearing surrounded by thorn bushes or scrub, the silhouette of distant trees etched against the dimming horizon. A single spark births a flame at the center, quickly growing into a warm fire that crackles and dances like an old friend. You can sense the hush, an anticipation that something crucial is about to unfold. In the Kalahari, an event like this might mark the beginning of a trance dance, a communal healing ceremony that can stretch through the night, culminating in dawn's soft light. Yet, in modern settings far from the desert's domain, we must adapt with care—using the best historical and ethnographic data to form an approximation of what the San call n/um tchai. We do not aim to replicate in a trivial sense but to pay homage, gleaning insights about communal connection, altered consciousness, and spiritual synergy. If possible, a San elder or recognized healer should guide or give permission; absent that, we proceed with humility, acknowledging that this ritual belongs foremost to the lineage that shaped it. Our contemporary version must remain faithful to the spirit, if not every detail. I have witnessed ceremonies where men and women from diverse backgrounds attempt the movements and chanting patterns, and I can testify that even a faint echo of the original power can be profoundly moving. However, we cannot overstate the importance of approaching as a learner. The vantage of "Ga!tzi N/um"—"Dance the Medicine (energy)"—is that we see ourselves not as consumers but as co-creators of a sacred container. If we proceed with seriousness, love, and communal goodwill, we can access a portion of that deep transformation the San describe. Let us also recall that a genuine San trance dancer may have trained over many years, forging a bond with the songs, steps, and intangible forces since childhood. Our momentary foray is but a respectful tribute. We must align each step with the qualities the San emphasize: respect for land, for the ancestors, for the animals, and for each participant's readiness. The aim is not a spectacle but a real merging of hearts. With that perspective, we can embark on an approximate blueprint—one that merges older knowledge with feasible modern adaptations.

AN OVERVIEW OF THE RITUAL FLOW

Below is a breakdown of major phases for "Ga!tzi N/um," from the initial spark of the fire at sunset to the final hush in which we express gratitude. Each stage is anchored in historical accounts while providing enough flexibility for modern practitioners to participate safely and meaningfully.

RITUAL STAGES AT A GLANCE

Sometimes it helps to visualize the flow in a simple chart.

Stage	Timing & Approx. Duration	Primary Activities
1. Preparation	Sunset - ~30 minutes	Gather in a circle, light fire, set intention, remove distractions
2. Grounding/ Chant	Next 15-20 minutes	Rhythmic clapping, simple medicine song, building synergy
3. Commencement	Follows chanting	Dancers stand, start slow steps around the fire
4. Building Energy	~20-30 minutes in	Increasing tempo, n/um activation, physical & emotional strain
5. Entering !Kia	When energy peaks	Deep trance, possible visions, first healing interactions
6. Healing Action	Continued trance state	Laying on hands, extracting negativity, communal synergy
7. Community Cleanse	Post individual healing	Group release of "star sickness," culminating in unifying outburst
8. Climactic Dance	Pre-dawn or final surge	Final intense round, abrupt stop, sacred silence
9. Recap & Close	Immediately after	Gratitude, shared reflections, gradual return to ordinary awareness

STEP-BY-STEP DETAILED EXPLANATION

1. **Preparation (Sunset)**

    The sun slides down the horizon, bathing the clearing in gold and amber. A hush settles as participants gather in a circular arrangement around a patch of ground chosen for safety and comfort. A fire crackles to life at the center, its tendrils of smoke curling skyward to carry prayers or intentions. In older San practice, men might go off to gather dry wood or bring in small offerings such as ostrich eggshells, while women tend the hearth. Yet, in a modern adaptation, roles can shift, provided we maintain a structure that places reverence above all. The primary circle might be the singers, forming a ring of support; the dancers stand outside or circle around them. Elders, or recognized facilitators, open the session by naming the purpose: it could be healing, personal transformation, or even communal harmony. One might say, "Let n/um flow in all of us," or if a San voice is present, they could speak a short phrase in Ju/'hoan or another relevant language. Bits of ostrich shell or small totems—shells, dried seeds, pieces of cloth—can be blessed and placed around the fire or tied to a sacred tree. This invites the spirits of ancestors, animals, and nature to watch over the night's proceedings. Participants remove watches, phones, flashy jewelry, letting their bodies come closer to an elemental state. In some reconstructions, men might don minimal attire or a short wrap; women might wear a cloth skirt or comfortable garments that allow for free movement. The notion is to adopt a sense of authenticity without veering into mere costuming. I once saw a workshop in which participants tried to copy exact !Kung outfits, but it felt forced. Instead, aim for simplicity, letting the body breathe. The designated healers, or "n/um kxao," may stand out by wearing a small pouch or bead that indicates their role. Others remain mindful that these healers will attempt to guide the group's energy. As the final glow of sunlight fades, everyone gathers in silence for a brief moment, each person forming an intention in their heart. One might think, "May I release negativity," or "Let me help heal the group." The clearing is still. Then a single voice might gently speak: "Kaia! tsa n/um... let the medicine come." Overhead, the first stars begin to peek through, reminding us that this dance is cosmic in scope. Each participant feels the warmth of the central fire, but also the subtle hush of night. The ground underfoot is stable yet slightly yielding, an apt metaphor for the journey ahead. This opening moment sets the tone: seriousness, humility, and a readiness to explore.

2. **Grounding and Chanting**

   A group of women or designated singers, seated near the fire, initiate a steady clapping—clap, clap, clap—perhaps three beats, then a pause, then three beats again, layering a basic polyrhythm to cradle the ceremony in sound.

3. **Further Expansion on Grounding/Chanting**

   Shortly after the clapping starts, one or two individuals begin a low hum, letting it expand into a tapestry of vocables that evoke the ancient medicine songs of the Kalahari. These might be as simple as "Aye... Aye... Aye..." repeated with gentle fluctuation, or something that faintly imitates Eland or Giraffe tunes. The key is not to mimic the exact lyrics—those are held by the San themselves—but to create a sense of layered synergy. If you have 10 participants, two or three might hold a continuous drone while another weaves a higher melodic line. Others might add soft exclamations: "Heh... heh... oh... oh..." at intervals. The polyrhythm of clapping becomes hypnotic, driving the circle's collective heartbeat. Those not actively singing or clapping can sway, letting their breath sync with the group. A rattle or two might join in, possibly homemade items with seeds or pebbles inside. The idea is that all participants contribute, forging a communal field of sound. This chanting phase can last 10 to 20 minutes or longer, depending on the group's comfort. If we recall the original vantage, the San see these songs as direct gifts from the divine realm. By sustaining the repetition, we invite energies beyond our everyday awareness. One might close their eyes or cast them to the fire, imagining the swirl of heat rising into the dark. The synergy often builds incrementally, intensifying in volume or speed, then dipping back. The leader or facilitator can encourage participants to keep it going: "Feel the rhythm in your stomach, let it come up through your chest." Gradually, tension melts and a sense of focus emerges. In the Kalahari, women's voices might ring out in falsetto, layering intricately. We can attempt a scaled-down version of that, mindful that the spiritual essence is more important than precise technique. By the end of this chant session, the circle is primed: hearts are beating faster, a shared field of intention is established, and the mind is readied for the next step: the actual dance.

4. **Commencement of Dance**
When the chanting has reached a stable groove, one or two designated healers stand, stepping forward around the fire. They might don ankle rattles or simply shift their weight from foot to foot in a measured shuffle. Everyone else maintains the song or clapping, but now the dancers become the focal point. Each step they take resonates with the pulse of the group, forging a living chain of movement and sound. At this moment, the boundary between watchers and dancers blurs—some participants may rise spontaneously to join the circle, while others remain singing.

5. **Building the Energy (N/um Activation)**
This phase can be exhilarating and intense. Over the course of 20 to 30

minutes, the dancers pick up speed. A small spiral might form, the line of dancers weaving closer to the fire and then outward again, symbolizing movement between the ordinary realm and the spirit domain. The seated singers follow the dancers with their eyes, adjusting volume or speed. If a dancer's footsteps accelerate, the claps match that energy. Sometimes, a spontaneous whoop or cry erupts from a dancer, signaling that the n/um in their belly is heating up. Lorna Marshall's accounts from the Kalahari speak of a distinct warmth or tingling in the pit of the stomach that climbs upward. Participants might grimace or breathe heavily, but they push on, for perseverance is crucial. The circle collectively acknowledges that physical strain is part of the crossing into trance. If you, as a modern participant, find yourself short of breath or fatigued, it's permissible to step back, rest for a moment, then rejoin if you feel called. The objective is to approach the threshold of exhaustion, which for the San is the gateway to altered consciousness. An elder or facilitator might walk among the dancers, softly patting their backs, whispering, "ǁGa, ǁga," or a similar phrase meaning "Let it come." This reassurance encourages dancers to keep going, trusting that the group's synergy will carry them. You may see participants start trembling or letting out short gasps. Their eyes might glaze over or fixate on the fire. These are normal signs that the boundary is shifting. If someone looks overwhelmed, a helper can guide them to sit momentarily, offering water or a gentle grounding hand. Meanwhile, the main group continues, relentlessly weaving the polyrhythm and chant. Energy rises in waves, each crest higher than the last. One dancer might fling their arms upward, shaking them as though releasing surging electricity. Another might let out a high-pitched moan, tears streaming. In the Kalahari, this raw display is accepted and expected, proof that n/um is indeed "boiling." That boiling leads to the next stage, crossing the threshold into what the San call !kia.

6. **Entering Trance (!Kia State)**
As the energy peaks, a select few dancers slip into deeper states, evidenced by subtle or dramatic signs: a glassy gaze, quivering limbs, or disassociated expressions. At this point, they are said to "have !kia," stepping beyond ordinary awareness into direct contact with spiritual or ancestral forces.

7. **Expanded Notes on Trance**
When the San speak of crossing into !kia, they describe seeing what ordinary sight cannot. Their vision might fill with luminous forms or ancestral faces. Some dancers claim a sense of traveling out of their bodies, glimpsing distant camps or hearing voices of the deceased. In a modern adaptation, participants might feel waves of heat, tingling, or an uncanny sense of presence nearby. If you are facilitating, gently

remind everyone that each person's experience is unique. Some might reach only a mild altered state, while others might slip surprisingly deep. Avoid pressuring anyone to exaggerate. Let the dance carry them naturally. If the group includes individuals trained in energy healing or bodywork, they can stand by to ensure physical safety—guiding those who falter from dizziness. In authentic Kalahari settings, it's said that a dancer in !kia could walk through flames or handle hot coals, though we must caution modern groups not to attempt such feats unless thoroughly prepared and truly in a safe, advanced state. Even the San approach that phenomenon with awe and care. If you see someone in a strong trance, you might notice their breath changes drastically—sometimes shallow and rapid, sometimes deep and slow. They might speak in half-words or spontaneously chant. At this point, we shift from the circle of dancing to the healing aspect. The newly trance-entranced dancer or designated "n/um kxao" can begin scanning participants for sickness or negativity. It's a fluid transition, guided by the group's awareness.

8. **Healing Interaction**

   The moment arises when a single dancer steps toward an individual who has requested healing (or is visibly in need). The rest of the circle continues to chant and clap, but perhaps lowers volume slightly to let the healer's actions stand out. Often, the healer places one hand on the person's chest and the other on their back, simulating extraction of dark energy. An abrupt shriek or exhalation might signal the final release, and the group collectively shouts or claps in unison to banish the sickness.

9. **Deeper Analysis of Healing Techniques**

   According to ethnographic accounts, the San conceptualize illness or negativity as a tangible, poisonous substance that can be plucked, sucked, or pulled from the body. The healer in deep trance might literally place their mouth on the person's chest, inhaling sharply, then spitting to the side or into the fire. A dramatic shriek often accompanies this final discard. People witnessing it sometimes recoil or gasp, but for the San, it signals a triumphant banishment of evil. Our modern reenactment can adapt this to personal comfort: if direct mouth contact is unwelcome, the healer can mime the motion, making the act just as symbolic. The effect is heightened by the group's continued chanting, which underscores the significance of the moment. Observers often report an electric hush right after the shriek, like an exclamation point in mid-air. Sometimes the healer staggers back, as though physically impacted by the extracted negativity. They might wave their arms, shaking them to fling off the residue. In older times, the San might have an Eland tail or piece of hide to wave as a further symbol. We might replicate it with a small piece of cloth. If multiple individuals need healing, the dancer or a second healer repeats the process, moving person to person. Each engagement is intense but relatively short. Overly long attempts can drain the healer or disrupt the group's rhythm. The circle, by adjusting the tempo of the chant, helps pace the sequence. Typically, an encouraging whoop or a sudden rise in volume can rally the healer if they appear fatigued. Meanwhile, bystanders or watchers keep the communal energy stable. One key point: in a real San context, the entire community invests emotional power in these gestures. It's not a performance but a group catharsis. We can maintain that dynamic by encouraging participants to hold genuine empathy, picturing the release of negativity from the person in question. If the participant feels a surge or shift, they can quietly confirm that sense of relief. The group might share a collective exhale or clap, reinforcing the healing's success.

10. **Community Cleansing**
    After personal extractions, the healer (or a group leader) might stand in the center and call upon the entire assembly to let go of "star sickness"—the envy, conflicts, or resentments overshadowing communal harmony. Everyone can join in a forceful exhalation or a wave of arms outward, as though flinging intangible pollutants into the darkness. A united shout or moment of loud clapping can finalize that group purge, leaving an aura of shared relief in its wake.

11. **Climactic Dance and Close**
    Now the circle transitions back to pure motion, forging a final climactic round of dance. The chanting might leap in tempo, the clapping intensifies, and any remaining rattle shakers push their instruments to a feverish pace. Whether it's midnight, 2 AM, or just an imagined pre-dawn, we capture the spirit of pressing on "until sunrise,"

akin to the San tradition. Some participants may be exhausted, sweat-soaked, hearts pounding, but they muster a last well of energy. Often in the Kalahari, the dance culminates right before daybreak. Here, we mimic that by letting the entire group unite in either stepping or stamping around the fire with as much vigor as they can muster. The songs soar to their highest pitch. The synergy can be exhilarating, even in a modern setting. Then, at a predetermined signal—maybe the lead singer raises a hand high or there's a sudden drumbeat—everything stops abruptly. The hush that follows is potent, as though the air itself vibrates. In that stillness, participants can literally feel a tingling in the body. Each breath is sharper, the mind is oddly calm yet alert. This quiet might linger for a good half-minute or longer, letting the residual energy settle. Then a soft communal hum or gentle humming round can provide a gentle landing. A facilitator or elder might murmur thanks to the spirits, to n/um, to the Eland or Mantis, or simply to the synergy that fueled the night. Everyone breathes in the hush, letting it cradle them in reflection.

12. **Recap and Sharing Circle**
Once the immediate hush disperses, people might gather around, sipping water or tea, and those who wish can share their experiences—perhaps glimpses of light, emotional releases, or subtle visions that surfaced during the dance.

13. **Tools and Gestures Recap**
All of this is anchored by a handful of key elements that deserve reiteration. First, the central fire, representing light, transformation, and the intangible link to spiritual realms. Flames can symbolize everything from divine presence to the shining core of the sun's energy. Second, the rattles or simple instruments—these carry the rhythmic force that stirs up the group's unity, helping to focus participants' minds on the beat rather than mental

chatter. Third, bodily adornments or subtle costume cues. We do not need to replicate every detail of San attire, but wearing a small token (a bead, a strip of leather) can help set intention and unify participants' sense of stepping into a sacred domain. Fourth, the cyclical formation: the ring of singers near the fire, the ring of dancers around that. Such geometry fosters cohesion, ensuring no one is left out or overshadowed. Fifth, the gestures of healing: sucking out the illness, flinging it away, shrieking out negativity, or gently massaging tension from someone's back or chest. Each is more than a random movement. In the San worldview, these gestures physically enact spiritual confrontation. Sixth, the impetus to keep going for hours, pushing past fatigue. Obviously, we must remain mindful of safety, but the principle stands: transformation often requires endurance. Seventh, the abrupt stop near dawn. This hallmark of the Kalahari trance dance locks in the spiritual work completed through the night. Eighth, the final acknowledgment and expression of gratitude. A communal hum or brief statement of thanks can anchor the sense of conclusion. Ninth, the group reflection time allows participants to process and integrate what they felt. Tenth, the moral dimension: dancing not for spectacle, but to unify hearts, release negativity, and welcome healing. Even if we only approximate the power the San harness, the framework itself can be profoundly moving. Eleventh, a reminder that attempts at advanced feats (like handling coals) must be approached with caution, if at all. Twelfth, recognition that real !kia is not achieved by simply panting for half an hour—true trance induction for the San is a lifetime practice. Thirteenth, acceptance that each participant will experience something unique, from mild relaxation to deep visions. Fourteenth, emphasis on group synergy. This is not an individualized, solitary journey but a shared wave of energy that lifts everyone. Fifteenth, the role of chanting. The layering of repeated syllables merges physical endurance with mental focus. Sixteenth, a reaffirmation that the environment sets the mood—dim lighting, presence of open sky, or at least symbolic references to nature. Seventeenth, the significance of each motion as an outward sign of an inner shift. Eighteenth, the seriousness with which negativity or "star sickness" is confronted. By truly naming it, we can transform it. Nineteenth, the role of humility in all participants. We are not "masters" of these energies but humble explorers. Twentieth, the sense that this is not a "one-off performance" but can be repeated over time to deepen communal bonds. Twenty-first, acknowledging that we are treading in sacred territory with an ancient lineage. Twenty-second, the possibility that small changes—like substituting certain instruments—do not necessarily break the ritual's authenticity if the spirit remains. Twenty-third, the knowledge that the real power rests in sincerity, not perfection. Twenty-fourth, disclaimers about not trivializing or monetizing the event without proper permission. Twenty-fifth, the ultimate goal: to glean a taste of the communal, healing, and cosmic dimension that defines San shamanism.

14. **Cautions for Modern Seekers**

Let us be forthright: this kind of dance can be physically demanding. People with health conditions should monitor themselves and stop if they feel dizzy or distressed. Drinking enough water, pacing one's breath, and learning to find a personal rhythm is crucial. Additionally, some participants may find intense emotional release—tears, sudden laughter, or memories bubbling up. That is natural and should be held in a supportive environment. We also highlight the necessity of a safe space, free from onlookers expecting a show. This is not about spectacle or a hurried "workshop highlight." Instead, approach it as a communal circle, ideally with no filming or outside interruption, so that participants feel free to express raw emotions. If you sense tension or conflict, address it beforehand. The dance can help release negativity, but it requires a baseline of trust among those present. Another caution: do not attempt to replicate the entire cultural matrix of the San. We do not presume to become "San shamans" in one night. Instead, see this as a respectful partial immersion that can deliver valuable insights about how communal movement and chant catalyze altered states. Minimizing or mocking any aspect would be disrespectful. For instance, the idea of wearing minimal clothing is not about exotic display but about comfort and tradition. If that's not feasible in your setting, adapt the principle while preserving dignity. In certain environments, a smaller circle or fewer participants might suffice. The main principle is shared intention and unwavering respect for the source tradition. Equally important: refrain from mixing random esoteric elements that might jar with the structure. If you want to incorporate your own spiritual beliefs, do so with gentleness, ensuring you do not overshadow the essential format described here.

15. **Potential Insights Gained**
Those who earnestly undergo even a fragment of this dance often report a heightened sense of unity, a new appreciation for communal healing, and a glimpse of how movement, chant, and spiritual willpower can merge to create profound shifts in perception.

16. **Conclusion on Ritual Reconstruction**
Standing at the edges of your own circle, you may realize that what began as an academic or spiritual experiment has ended as a lived revelation: a taste of that intangible fire the San call n/um. You notice how your skin tingles, how your heart resonates with the group's collective beat, how the swirling energy in the circle has carried you to a calmer, more open vantage of yourself and your companions.

Such an outcome speaks to the extraordinary capacity of humans to connect through a shared rhythm, singing, and the harnessing of intangible forces. If performed with sincerity, love, and the humility to learn, the "Ga!tzi N/um" approach can become a highlight of communal exploration. Yet it must never be exploited as a sideshow or a tourist attraction without the input of the tradition's rightful custodians. The San have weathered centuries of upheaval, clinging to this practice as a key to their social health and spiritual identity. We owe them gratitude for showing that even in an environment as harsh as the Kalahari, or as modern as a city loft, people can evoke archaic, primal energies for mutual benefit. Each gesture—the shuffle of feet, the placing of hands over someone's chest, the final shout scattering negativity to the sky—has depth. Where the outside world sees quaint ritual, the San see a gateway to the spirit world. Where some might see sweaty chaos, the San see a galvanizing wave that unites the community against sickness and discord. The value is incalculable, partly because it is intangible. Modern seekers who embrace these teachings might also learn to honor them by crediting the source, inviting indigenous voices, and ensuring that any adaptation remains grounded in respect. If you are leading a group, emphasize that the journey is internal as well as communal: participants should attune to sensations, remain present, and support each other rather than compete. The dance's success is measured not by a perfect re-creation of specific lyrics or steps, but by the sincerity of mutual healing. By the time the final hush falls, it can feel as though an entire night's worth of tension has dissolved. People often remark on a lightness or clarity that lingers for days. Indeed, that is the legacy of this ancient knowledge: an invitation to discover that we can transform pain into communal strength, that the boundary between mundane and miraculous is thinner than we suspect. It also underscores that we must remain humble as we borrow from a culture with thousands of years of history. The foot-stomping circle, at its best, reveals the universal human capacity for trance, for forging mystical bonds through sound and motion. And it reminds us that the planet on which we dance is alive with powers and presences we barely understand. The next time you see a dim glow of flame in the twilight, or hear the faint pulse of rhythmic clapping, let the memory of this dance call you home to the oldest parts of our shared humanity. The step-by-step instructions are only signposts. What you truly glean depends on your openness, your readiness to surrender to the circle, and your willingness to walk carefully on a path that is both venerable and vulnerable. May your circle be honest, may your hearts sync in communal spirit, and may your own n/um rise gracefully to illuminate the darkness. In this way, we honor not just the San, but the living bond between human bodies, ancestral voices, and the environment that cradles us. That synergy, discovered anew each time, is what keeps the spark of ancient shamanic wisdom alive across millennia and across continents.

Shamanic Universals

I have often felt a sense of awe when contemplating how two peoples so distant—like the San of southern Africa and the Aboriginal Australians—could share remarkable threads in their spiritual tapestries. It reminds me of standing under starry skies in the Kalahari one month, then finding myself under that vast Australian night on another occasion, both times feeling the pulse of an ancient presence in the land. Part of me wonders whether, in the dawn of humanity, we all carried the seeds of a fundamental shamanic worldview that blossomed differently across continents. When I read about Dreamtime stories in Arnhem Land or about Mantis and Eland among the San, I detect a common note: a deep reverence for the land as alive, for animals as kin, and for invisible forces that shape us. This is the chord that resonates between these traditions: a perception that the universe is full of spirits, that a sacred time of creation still underpins reality, and that through trance or dream, one can step back into that power.

  Anyone who has traveled among Aboriginal communities, even briefly, may notice how central the Dreamtime remains to their identity, how the land is not just physical ground but a repository of ancestral journeys. The Dreamtime, also referred to as the Dreaming, is often described as "everywhen" —a concept meaning that the world was formed by mythical beings that still exist in spiritual form, and that time itself can fold or blend so that the past creation events continue to guide the present. Meanwhile, across an ocean and eons of separate development, the San speak of the earliest era when humans and animals were not yet distinct. A time when Eland, Mantis, or other figures roamed side by side with early people, forging a world that was fluid, shape-shifting, and permeable between spirit and matter. These stories, told around fires in both deserts, ring with a common truth: that the physical environment is not inert but animated by living story and spirit presence.

I recall hearing a San elder relate how in the first creation, all beings could speak to each other, and only after a subsequent separation did humans lose some of that direct connection. If you look at certain Aboriginal accounts, you find that ancestral beings traveled the land, singing it into form, leaving behind evidence of their shape-shifting presence in rocks or waterholes. To the outsider, these might seem "myths," but for the people who uphold them, they are living truths encoded in the land itself. When I learned about the Rainbow Serpent that shaped the rivers and mountains in some Aboriginal traditions, my mind jumped to the Mantis that conjured the first Eland from honey, or the so-called rain animal of the San that could bring storms.

Both sets of stories place a powerful, often non-human or hybrid figure at the heart of creation, merging nature's force with a deity's persona. Such parallels speak less of direct contact—since these societies evolved separately—and more of universal patterns in how humans interpret cosmic mysteries.

The concept of animism provides a big piece of that puzzle. In both the Australian bush and the Kalahari, communities historically lived intimately with the land, depending on natural cues for survival. When a group depends wholly on reading tracks, gathering water, interpreting animal behavior, and sensing subtle climate shifts, there emerges a worldview in which every element is animated by significance. For the San, trees might harbor spirits, waterholes might be guarded by serpentine beings, and dead ancestors might watch from the stars. For Aboriginal Australians, certain rocks or hills are the transformed bodies of Dreamtime beings, while specific animals are clan totems linking families to spiritual lineages. In each case, the boundary between person, animal, and landscape is not so rigid as in many modern Western frameworks. One might say this is the hallmark of an animistic cosmos: everything is alive, vibrant, and interrelated, with spiritual essence saturating the material.

That sense of a "mythic time" accessible even now helps each culture maintain continuity. The Dreamtime, as often explained, is not just a period in the past, but an ongoing dimension. The ancestral beings who formed the rivers or carved out certain mountains remain present in those features, or in the sky as stars, ready to communicate with those who know how to listen. In the Kalahari, the notion is that a trance dance reverts the group to the First Creation, letting them harness the original healing power that emerged when humans and animals were still one. It's a cyclical renewal. So both societies practice or practiced community rites that reaffirm the primal bond: a corroboree in Australia might reenact the journeys of the Rainbow Serpent or the Kangaroo ancestor, while a San healing dance enacts the unity of n/um in all living things. One can see a resonance: communal singing, communal motion, and the shared recapitulation of cosmic creation stories.

Another striking parallel arises in the realm of shamanic practice. The San have their trance dance, an all-night affair of rhythmic clapping, singing, and dancing, culminating in healers extracting illness or negative forces from the community. Meanwhile, Aboriginal Australians have ceremonies where the didgeridoo's droning, accompanied by clapsticks, can induce a group trance. I heard an account of Aboriginal "clever men" who literally suck illness out of patients, then spit it away—almost identical to how a San healer might "pull out" the sickness with a dramatic shriek. One might see this across the planet in shamanic cultures, but it is especially fascinating that the motifs (the communal circle, the driving music, the interplay of dreams or visions, the direct confrontation with an invisible cause of disharmony) line up so closely. At times, Aboriginal ceremonies involve painting the body with designs that represent Dreamtime beings, while San dancers might wear a headband or an Eland tail to invoke that animal's potency. Even the so-called "playing with fire" that some shamans do—walking on coals, handling embers—crops up in both traditions. One may interpret such feats as demonstrations of the trance state's power or proof of divine protection.

I recall speaking with an Aboriginal friend who described how, during a corroboree, dancers adopt the "skin" of ancestral spirits. That reminded me uncannily of how a San shaman in trance might say "I have become the Eland," describing the moment they feel the animal's spirit take over. Both speak to shape-shifting or merging with a totemic presence. Another universal phenomenon is the role of dreams. For Aboriginal people, the Dreamtime name itself indicates that dreams are more than random mental images: they're portals to the ancestors and the primal creative state. Similarly, among the San, certain myths are said to be gleaned in dreams, or a healer might solve a community problem by dreaming the solution. In each case, the boundary between dream and waking reality is not fixed. A vision seen in a dream might be as authoritative as a direct conversation.

One cannot help but see the possibility that these parallels reflect an ancient, universal layer of human consciousness: the capacity for ritual, trance, and symbolic creation. Scholars sometimes argue that shamanism was likely humanity's earliest form of spiritual practice, emerging before agriculture or settled life. If that's the case, then the San, who represent among the oldest genetic lineages in Africa, and the Aboriginal Australians, among the first out-of-Africa migrants, could both be carrying forward the legacy of that primal tradition. Even though they parted ways tens of thousands of years ago, their separate evolutions might have retained the core patterns of animism, communal trance, healing through spirit interaction, and an underlying cosmogony that sees the land itself as shaped by mythic beings. It's a goosebump-inducing idea: that maybe a very early Homo sapiens tradition was "carried" in seeds around the world, later diversifying but still recognizable in the San's Eland dances and the Aboriginal corroborees.

To be sure, we must avoid romantic oversimplification. Aboriginal cultures are hugely diverse, with hundreds of language groups and variations in myth. Not all groups hold large communal trance dances: some might rely more on personal vision quests, or local site-based ceremonies. The San, too, are not a monolith, although the trance dance is widespread among them. The nature of the myths also differs: Kaggen the Mantis is a trickster figure who often stumbles or plays pranks, whereas many Aboriginal Dreamtime stories are more solemn, though they can have comedic elements as well. Another difference: in parts of Australia, the didgeridoo is essential for ceremony, along with clapsticks and body paintings that can be quite elaborate. Among the San, the triggers for trance are primarily the polyphonic clapping, the rattles, the stamping, and occasionally the presence of n/um-laden objects. As for psychoactive substances, certain Aboriginal groups use mild plant additives, though not always. The San typically rely on hyperventilation and movement alone—no strong entheogens—yet the effect is equally potent.

But these differences do not overshadow the underlying parallels: that the land is storied, that animal or ancestral spirits remain accessible, and that healing is not just physical but social and spiritual. I recall a Ju/'hoan elder emphasizing that if someone grows too proud, they lose the empathy needed to keep the dance going. That reminds me of the Aboriginal ethic that humans are custodians, not masters, of the land: if they break the law of the Dreamtime, disharmony follows. Both are moral teachings that revolve around humility and mutual care, a hallmark of these older foraging-based cultures. Indeed, the notion of "insulting the meat" among the San—where a successful hunter must downplay their kill to avoid arrogance—mirrors the modesty we see in many Aboriginal communities, where sharing and mutual obligation are cornerstones.

Art also emerges as a crucial conduit of spiritual expression in both traditions. The San's cave paintings, with those iconic half-animal trance dancers or Eland images, exhibit a remarkable synergy of symbolism and daily life. Aboriginal rock or cave paintings, and also their sand drawings or bark paintings, revolve around Dreamtime tracks, ancestral journeys, and totemic stories. Dotted patterns, concentric circles, or stylized animals can represent "songlines," the routes the ancestors traveled during creation. That motif resonates strongly with the San paintings that incorporate cracks in the rock to show spirit portals or ephemeral shapes that dancers might witness in trance. Both sets of art often operate on multiple levels: a literal depiction of an animal, a symbolic representation of intangible power, and a map of mythical events that shaped the environment. In some sense, each painting is a gateway for connecting with the spirit world.

It's mesmerizing to realize that genetic studies identify the San and Aboriginal Australians as two of the oldest continuous human lineages. They are like bookends of an epic story. The ancestors of the Aboriginal Australians left Africa maybe 50,000 to 60,000 years ago, carrying an early cultural package with them that developed into the Dreamtime worldview. Meanwhile, the San remained in Africa, refining a parallel set of shamanic beliefs. Today, we see echoes of that ancient substrate in the foot-stomping dance or the corroboree, in references to Kaggen or the Rainbow Serpent, in shape-shifting myths, in the bridging of dream and waking. The continents parted, the people parted, but the universal essence of animistic shamanism thrived in each location. The date of that initial diaspora is staggering: if we consider that the Dreamtime approach in Australia and the trance dance approach in southern Africa are both living traditions, then we are witnessing two living conduits to a primeval human spiritual stratum.

Such insights can enliven the discussions around shamanism worldwide. For those of us who grew up in cultures far removed from these contexts, it can be revelatory to see how "exotic" or "archaic" practices from opposite ends of the world line up so well. It suggests that the impetus to commune with spirits through dance, to see the land as shaped by mythical transformations, is a near-universal human inheritance. By paralleling the San's First Creation with the Aboriginal Dreamtime, we glimpse that humans consistently conceive of a time before the present boundaries, a time of shapeshifting potential. Shamans in both realms are essentially the keepers of that memory, bridging the old epoch with the now.

Of course, I do not wish to flatten the distinctiveness of each culture. The Dreamtime is a richly codified concept, linking every site and clan to a specific story or ancestor. The San do not systematically label every rock or waterhole with a creation tale in the same manner (though certain sites have strong significance). Also, Aboriginal Australians have intricately layered kinship rules and clan structures related to totems that may outstrip anything we see among the San. In some Aboriginal groups, extensive genealogies tie people to the Dreamtime being that fathered or mothered their lineage. The San, with their egalitarian ethos, do not typically break up into named totemic clans, though they do hold in common a reverence for the Eland or Mantis. Another difference: in some Aboriginal contexts, large-scale gatherings across multiple groups might occur for ceremonies, whereas the San typically live in smaller bands. But these structural variations do not negate the broader parallels in shamanic worldview.

The same is true regarding environment. The Kalahari is known for aridity, dramatic temperature swings, reliance on wild plant foods, and the presence of iconic animals like the Eland, giraffe, lion, or gemsbok. In Australia, the environment can vary from tropical coasts to deserts, with a range of fauna such as kangaroos, emus, or the barramundi fish. Each environment influences the shape of myths and the style of ritual. Yet, the deeper pattern remains: both sets of societies require a nuanced reading of the land, treat certain animals as more than just prey or neighbors, and revolve communal gatherings around upholding the cosmic relationships established in "mythic time."

In a broader sense, the resilience of both these cultures despite colonial intrusions and modern pressures is also worth highlighting. The San have endured displacement, forced settlement, and cultural appropriation; Aboriginal Australians have faced dispossession, stolen generations, the fracturing of language groups, and more. Yet, in many enclaves, they keep dancing, keep telling stories, keep painting, keep teaching. These living traditions speak of an ongoing capacity to adapt while safeguarding the spiritual core. If a modern student or spiritual seeker truly wants to understand shamanic wisdom, it is crucial to do so with recognition of the historical injustices these people have faced, ensuring that we approach them not as museum curiosities but as living guardians of some of humanity's most profound heritage.

Sometimes, I hear people marvel that "the San do a trance dance just like the Aboriginal corroboree," or "They both talk about dreaming and shape-shifting." They might leap to the conclusion that there must have been contact across the Indian Ocean, or that some ancient mariners carried the secrets back and forth. Anthropologically, that's highly unlikely. The more convincing explanation is that these are parallel evolutions or a reflection of a deeper universal shamanic structure that was set in motion long before migrations scattered humans to the ends of the Earth. In other words, the wellsprings of collective chanting, dancing, dream-based myth, and animistic imagination might lie in our shared human mind.

In my own travels, I find it endlessly enchanting to see the same motifs rise in different settings. Whether in the Kalahari or in a remote part of Australia, someone points to a rock outcrop and says "That used to be a spirit who shaped the land." Or they mention that in older times, humans and animals were not separate species. Or they speak of dancing all night until the boundary dissolves and they can see the face of the ancestors. These are the intangible threads of a universal heritage that probably goes back tens of thousands of years. In these threads, we find the seeds of empathy toward nonhuman life, the impetus for communal healing, and the recognition that existence is layered with hidden dimensions.

We might also glean lessons for our modern age. Both the San and many Aboriginal peoples maintain that living lightly on the land, taking only what is needed, and respecting the unseen spiritual guardians fosters balance. The acts of sharing, humility, and cyclical gathering in ceremony reinforce social cohesion. We are a species that thrives when we periodically gather to sing, dance, and unify our hearts. The San foot-stomping circle is not so different from the corroboree in that sense: a group conjures a shared rhythm to transcend daily frictions and align with a cosmic or ancestral source. And so, if we compare them, we see that both societies managed for millennia to sustain small-scale, egalitarian structures without depleting their resources or losing the spark of awe for the environment. Not that life was idyllic or free of conflict, but the spiritual frameworks helped maintain a sense of belonging and accountability to the land.

I sometimes joke that the ancient travelers who left Africa may have carried the "drumbeat gene" or the "shamanic vibe" with them, but it's less about literal genetics and more about the universal capacity for humans to craft spiritual meaning from nature's mysteries. The fact that the San and Aboriginal Australians remain living exemplars of that capacity is profoundly important. They are living proof that deep spiritual traditions can persist across unimaginable time spans. For those who wish to learn from them, humility is paramount. Understanding that we are glimpsing a legacy that is ours in a broader, human sense, yet belongs most directly to the communities that nurtured it.

We do well to salute these parallels: an emphasis on cyclical time, the presence of an animating creation period that can be revisited, the central role of communal ceremony in bridging tangible and intangible, the practice of shape-shifting or soul-flight by specialists, the integration of visual art with myth, the moral teaching of humility and sharing, the interplay of dream and waking, and a cosmic worldview that sees stars, animals, waterholes, and people as part of a single tapestry. All of that, in some sense, points to a primal heritage.

When we marvel at the archaic rock art of the Drakensberg or Tsodilo Hills, with dancing figures merging into animal forms, we might recall the Aboriginal rock art sites that show Wandjina with huge eyes and no mouths, signifying cloud or rain spirits. In each place, the painting on the wall is not just decorative. It's a portal. It's a reaffirmation of continuity between the mythic realm and the daily realm. Anthropologists sometimes talk of "the entoptic phenomena in shamanic art," which might be universal neurological patterns under trance. Others talk of "songlines" in Australia or "power lines" in San contexts, implying lines of spiritual force. However we label it, the deeper reality is that humans have historically sought ways to link their ephemeral existence to the creative wellspring that formed the cosmos.

In reflecting on all this, I come away feeling that the Dreamtime is not exclusively Australian, nor is the San's trance-based First Creation exclusively African. They are local expressions of a universal approach: that by chanting, dancing, and telling stories, we actively participate in creation. We carry on the impetus begun in those earliest days when shapes were not fixed, when we had the power to dream ourselves anew. Indeed, if the Aboriginal say "the Dreaming is now," the San might say "through !kia, we see the old times renewed." Each phrase points to the same truth: spiritual power dwells in the interplay of mythic memory and present communal action.

It humbles me to know that despite the ravages of colonial history, these traditions survive. The San continue to hold their all-night healing dances, even if many have been relocated or integrated into other societies. Aboriginal Australians still maintain corroborees, Dreamtime stories, and complex land-based traditions, even though they too face modern challenges. Their resilience testifies that these ways of relating to the world address fundamental human needs, such as the need for communal identity, moral coherence, healing, and a bond with the land's living tapestry.

In sum, while the San and Aboriginal Australians may not have direct historical contact, the parallels in their spiritual beliefs and practices shine with a clarity that suggests either an extremely ancient common root or the repeated convergence of human societies on the same archetypal truths. Each approach underscores that the line between the everyday and the sacred is permeable. Each teaches that we can enter "mythic time," that the land speaks, that animals are our kin, that ceremony transforms conflict into harmony, and that dreams or trance can yield real knowledge. Observing these parallels isn't about diminishing the uniqueness of each culture, but about celebrating our shared capacity for wonder and transformation.

To me, it's like seeing two mirrors face each other across the globe, each reflecting a piece of the earliest soul of humanity. One might call that soul "the Dreaming," or "the First Creation," or anything else. But the essence is that when humans turn inward and outward simultaneously—toward their own spiritual depths and toward nature's silent grandeur—something universal emerges. A synergy of story, song, and survival that we call shamanism. A synergy that insists that none of us are alone: we walk among ancestors, among spirits, and among living patterns that began at the dawn of time.

And so, if you look at the band of Ju/'hoansi singing around a fire late into the night, or if you watch an Aboriginal clan painting themselves in white ochre under the blazing stars, you may glimpse the same primal glow in their eyes. A glow that says the land is alive, that existence is pregnant with meanings, that the right dance or the right chant can open doors to the creative wellspring. That's the resonance between the

Kalahari's trance dance and the Australian corroboree: a universal thread of human spirituality, reminding us that beneath the differences of language and geography, there's a shared impetus to worship, heal, and understand.

One day, perhaps, we'll see more collaborative events where Aboriginal elders and San elders share experiences, bridging their cultural contexts to note the similarities of their ceremonies. It would be a meeting of living ancient lineages, each offering reflections on how humankind once lived in a reciprocity with the environment. Maybe they would speak of how the Milky Way is the path of the old ones, how certain snakes or insects hold cosmic significance, how dancing can banish sickness or conjure rainfall. Maybe they would realize that, yes, these are universal songs that have been echoing since people first stood upright and gazed at the night sky in wonder. Perhaps that synergy could spark new forms of mutual support, cross-continental wisdom, and deeper recognition of how valuable these traditions remain in a modern world so often starved for communal ritual and ecological reverence.

Ultimately, even if such a grand meeting never happens, we as observers can learn from both. Studying the San's intimacy with n/um and the Aboriginal deep knowledge of Dreamtime can expand our sense of what it means to be human. It can teach us about the healing power of communal song, the moral dimension of humility, the practice of seeing land as impregnated with story. We may never live as foragers in those deserts ourselves, but we can glean a sense of how ancient societies thrived with minimal hierarchy, forging social ties through shared spiritual events. That knowledge is precious, especially at a time when so many modern societies search for ways to reconnect with nature, rediscover communal ties, or find holistic solutions to mental and spiritual malaise.

In the end, the parallels between the San and Aboriginal Australians stand as living proof that humanity, at its deepest root, has always sought to fuse myth with daily life. Both groups exemplify that "mythic time" can be touched in the here and now, through the embodied, rhythmic acts of ceremony. Their ancestors sang the world into being, and they keep singing. Their shamans or elders journey into unseen realms for healing, and they keep dancing. And behind it all is a cosmic assertion: that the world is alive, that we are never alone, that creation is not a one-time event but an ongoing interplay. When we hold that perspective, we find ourselves resonating with the same cosmic chord, no matter which desert we stand in.

Shakti Beauregard

Sunset

Shamanic wisdom, like any deep current, has a way of reappearing when we need it most. In my experience, the profound teachings of the San people illuminate that ancient current better than many, acting as a reminder that something quietly enduring has underpinned human existence for countless generations. It isn't simply about "primitive" ritual or some quaint relic from a distant past. Rather, the San traditions show a living, breathing tapestry of healing, spirituality, social cohesion, and intimate dialogue with the cosmos. At times, I marvel at the expansiveness of their worldview: how it embraces both daily practicalities—finding water, forging unity in a tight-knit band—and the mysteries of how existence came to be. Listening to an older Ju/'hoan woman describe a nighttime dance, you might feel that all the hustle and fragmentation of the contemporary world melts away. In its place stands a vision of life braided together by shared ceremony, mythic depth, and a fierce regard for nature's sacredness.

The worldview of the San, as we have explored, is not about naive illusions. It is an intricate framework that addresses the layers of body, mind, society, and spirit in a single stroke. The healing dances that swirl under the Kalahari stars do not just ease individual maladies but also quell social tensions and reorient the community's spiritual bearings. Their mythic figures like Kaggen (the Mantis) convey a playful yet powerful sense of how cosmic forces intersect with everyday living. Rock paintings reveal an art form that merges material reality with transcendent visions. And the languages themselves—steeped in delicate clicks that express nuance beyond direct translation—carry centuries upon centuries of unwritten knowledge. When we look beyond popular stereotypes of the "Bushman" as a hapless primitive, we find an astute philosophical tradition that recognizes intangible realities and employs them for very tangible healing. This deeper look compels us to reassess what we have dismissed or overlooked in the so-called simple cultures of the world.

I have long suspected that one reason people are drawn to the San tradition is that we sense a missing element in our own frantic existence. We see glimpses of ancient wholeness: a method of addressing sickness that sees no separation between mind and body, or between the individual and the group. We recall that the healing trance dance does not isolate a "patient" in a sterile room. Instead, it activates an entire circle of participants, ignites bodily energy, and fosters emotional release. We also encounter that readiness to laugh at trickster gods who sometimes bungle, reminding us of humility. It is no exaggeration to say that in societies so riddled with anxiety, mental fragmentation, and longing for meaning, these old ways strike a resonant chord.

Yet, one of the most important lessons from the San is that no matter how impressive or compelling these teachings are, they emerge from a living people with a history of dispossession, marginalization, and struggle. Their precarious present includes displacement from ancestral land, language erosion, and misrepresentation in mainstream media, among many other pressures. For their communities, preserving the trance dance or continuing to speak the old clicks is not an abstract preference but a matter of cultural survival and spiritual continuity. We, as students or admirers from other worlds, must therefore tread carefully and ethically, remembering that the best knowledge does not belong to everyone by default. It arises from particular lineages—people who have carried it through tribulations. Their perspective, their permission, and their benefit remain central if we wish to respectfully learn or adapt anything.

I have stood at public events where I've seen a watered-down performance labeled a "Bushman dance" made to amuse tourists.

The dancers seemed exhausted, bored, or perhaps resigned to treat the night as a show for outsiders. Compared to the immersive ceremonies described by anthropologists in earlier decades, or even in remote enclaves today, these staged spectacles do not reflect the full depth. One wonders if the watchers who clap politely have any inkling of the cosmic significance the dance once held. This mismatch exemplifies the pitfalls of appropriation: when a practice or symbol is ripped out of its context and paraded as entertainment. Is it better that we see some representation and not let it vanish entirely, or is it worse because it becomes an empty shell?

Plenty of contemporary voices among the San themselves have pointed out the dangers of such a path. They caution that not all visitors approach with genuine respect. Some adopt a phrase like "n/um energy" to spice up a workshop or a brand of holistic health, failing to note that n/um is embedded in a collective social fabric where intangible power is recognized but also regulated by elders, communal norms, and ritual parameters (Cultural-Survival.org). One cannot simply pluck the concept from that setting, rename it for marketing, and expect to preserve its authenticity or avoid harming the source culture. But that does not mean cross-cultural sharing is impossible. On the contrary, the San's worldview can be a gift to the wider world if we pursue it ethically, acknowledging the tradition's custodians. Collaboration that respects intellectual property, shares financial benefits, and invites indigenous oversight can lead to beneficial cultural exchange (SouthAfrica.co.za). A healthy example is a workshop or festival where real San elders are present, explaining the dance's meaning, demonstrating it as they see fit, and ensuring that participants treat it with gravity. A far cry from bootleg versions of "Bushman ceremonies" offered by outsiders for quick profit.

While these issues may seem specific to the San, they mirror broader patterns wherever indigenous knowledge meets modern hunger for novelty. The universal craving for "exotic spirituality" can blind us to the truth that these traditions are real lifeways, not tourist attractions or shamanic amusements. I have seen well-meaning spiritual seekers adopt bits of "spirit animal" references but drop the communal or ecological dimension that is so crucial to the original context. Meanwhile, the underlying ethic that the San observe—like how a healer must remain humble, or how the entire group cooperates to maintain social balance—gets lost in translation. The problem is not that modern seekers are malicious, but that ignorance or superficial interest can degrade something that took thousands of years to refine.

Let us note, though, that the potential for beneficial cross-cultural exchange remains. If we engage with the San's perspective in good faith, we find that it underlines universal messages about empathy, humility, communal care, and respect for nature. So many people today rediscover the importance of mind-body unity, acknowledging the psychosomatic aspects of illness, or the need for group support in mental health contexts. The San have been practicing these integrated approaches for millennia without the aid of modern science or pharmaceuticals. Instead, they rely on communal synergy, the deep stirrings of music, the harnessing of n/um, and mythic frameworks that prevent isolation and despair. When we truly absorb that lesson, we realize it is not archaic at all, but forward-thinking—a blueprint for how communities might restore mental and emotional well-being in a hyper-individualized era.

Another notable dimension is the egalitarian nature of their spirituality. Many religious systems revolve around specialized priests or hierarchical structures, restricting access to transformative states. Among the San, multiple men and women can train in healing. The capacity to harness n/um is not the province of a singular priestly caste but a skill open to those with the dedication and inclination. That openness fosters a sense of shared responsibility: if sickness afflicts one person, the entire community invests in the healing process. It also democratizes spiritual power. For people outside the San tradition, this is a profound reminder that spirituality does not always require an intermediary or an institution, but can be nurtured by shared cultural practice. If one is determined to learn from this, it means creating communal structures that invite everyone into the circle rather than relegating them to passive observation.

Modern society's interest in "alternate states" sometimes veers into chemical solutions—psychedelic substances, for instance. Meanwhile, the San show that bodily movement, chant, and the mutual will to heal can induce states of expanded consciousness without external substances. This approach resonates with contemporary explorations of breathwork, ecstatic dance, and related somatic practices. The difference is that for the San, these states are woven into the entire cultural matrix, complete with moral guidelines, mythic instructions, and a shared sense of accountability. It isn't a quick fix or an isolated weekend experience. It is part of ongoing life, repeated monthly or more often, allowing the community to self-regulate tension, reaffirm social bonds, and reclaim spiritual vitality.

Still, the real question is not only how non-San individuals can glean personal inspiration, but how we might support and uplift the San themselves. They continue to live in circumstances that hamper free expression of their ancient ways. Land dispossession prevents many from returning to the wide ranges where they once roamed and held all-night dances. Alcohol abuse and poverty weigh heavily, fracturing the sense of continuity that once passed seamlessly from elder to youth (CulturalSurvival.org). Government policies may or may not be conducive to them resuming a forager lifestyle. Missions or mainstream education systems can inadvertently or deliberately erode the old languages. Thus, while we marvel at their heritage, the living carriers of that heritage need tangible recognition, legal rights to their territory, educational support that includes mother-tongue instruction, and so forth. If we truly value their "shamanic secrets," we cannot ignore these socio-political realities. Preserving the intangible requires safeguarding the conditions in which it thrives.

As a scholar or seeker, referencing the San means acknowledging that we rely on anthropological, historical, and indigenous sources that have documented their stories (SouthAfrica.co.za; CulturalSurvival.org). We do not invent or glamorize. We rely on testimonies from individuals like =Oma Djo, who famously stated, "Our n!ore is who we are" (CulturalSurvival.org), capturing in simple words how the land—n!ore—is inseparable from identity. A concept that deep does not belong in a fleeting pop article. It calls for deep reflection on how environment shapes the soul, how displacement severs a spiritual bond. The same reflection might prompt us to examine our relationships with our own homelands, the ways we might re-sanctify local landscapes, or the urgency of halting ecological destruction. The times we live in, overshadowed by climate crises and social fragmentation, might desperately need the example of a people who found equilibrium in seemingly inhospitable desert conditions for countless generations.

  I find it particularly moving that even in the early 19th-century transcriptions by Bleek and Lloyd, or in more recent fieldwork, the San reveal a flair for metaphor that transcends cultural boundaries. The image of a blind healer who says God keeps his eyeballs in a bag until the trance moment underscores a universal truth about how deeper vision arises from an interior transformation. A purely rational mind might scoff, but many spiritual explorers or psychologists would recognize a core metaphor: we cannot see the deeper layers of reality until we shift states. In an era dominated by science and rationality, it's easy to dismiss invisible realms or intangible energies. The San quietly demonstrate that there is more than one way to acquire knowledge, that direct experience can surpass intellectual speculation. That is not to say we must abandon rational inquiry; rather, we supplement it with a willingness to explore altered consciousness and the communal dimensions of healing.

All of this, of course, stands or falls on whether we approach the San tradition with sincerity. If we treat it merely as an anthropological footnote, we lose the living impetus that has guided them for centuries. If we exploit it or commercialize it in a shallow manner, we do them a disservice and dilute the potential lessons. So the onus is on each of us, whether scholar, traveler, teacher, or casual reader, to maintain that threshold of respect. We might read the stories in academic monographs or watch documentary clips on the trance dance, but we remain aware that behind the text or camera lens are real families, real communities, whose spiritual realm is not a novelty but an everyday anchor.

I have often concluded that the real gift the San offer is a renewed sense of wonder at the capacity of the human mind, body, and heart to unify in the face of hardship. Their ecstatic healing dances run from dusk to dawn precisely because the hardest transitions—sickness, envy, grief—require concentrated communal effort. They do not try to solve them with brief prayers or personal introspection alone. Instead, they harness the synergy of rhythmic singing, the bodily strain of dancing, the powerful imagery of ancestral myths, and the sharp boundary-crossing of trance. This synergy yields a relief that is simultaneously physical, emotional, spiritual, and social. In so doing, they teach us about ways to approach integrated healing that surpass standard Western compartments of "medical," "psychological," or "religious." For them, it is all one process, as natural as breathing, as essential as water in the desert.

It makes sense, then, that modern practitioners in fields like transpersonal psychology or community therapy look to the San for insights. They see in that single ceremony an approach that addresses an entire community's wellness. The individual is not alone in their affliction; the group takes it on collectively, harnessing intangible energies that Western discourse might label symbolic or psychosomatic. Yet, whether we interpret n/um as literal spiritual power or psychosomatic effect does not reduce the significance that it works for them. In many cases, the results speak for themselves in terms of emotional relief and group cohesion. By bridging intellectual rigor and spiritual openness, we can appreciate these practices without imposing a reductive lens. They can remain mystical, powerful, and real, even if we do not fully understand or replicate their processes.

There is also a radical egalitarian note in the San tradition that resonates with modern movements against social hierarchies. The "insulting the meat" custom, in which a hunter is teased about his catch to avoid pride, underscores a method of preventing power imbalances. That custom is intimately tied to their spiritual ethic: arrogance disrupts communal harmony and can stir negative forces. We see echoes of this ethic in the healing dance, where many people can become healers, and no single figure holds an exclusive claim on spiritual authority. This approach fosters resilience: if a recognized healer falls ill or passes away, others can step in. Meanwhile, the group is never reliant on a sole charismatic figure, ensuring collective agency. Western societies might glean something from this approach, considering how easily we succumb to hierarchy or hero-worship in spiritual domains.

Some might ask how this entire conversation about preserving San ways and approaching them respectfully fits into the 21st-century context of globalization, digital connectivity, and accelerating environmental crises. The answer, to me, is that preserving these intangible heritages has never been more crucial. In a rapidly homogenizing world, we risk losing unique vantage points on what it means to be human. If the San vanish—either physically or culturally—the planet loses not just a small group, but a living link to the earliest chapters of human spiritual exploration. We lose the demonstration of a society that integrated healing and communal ethics seamlessly. We lose an approach to life that, for all its challenges, sustains joy and belonging in an often harsh environment. We lose a reminder that the mind can reach astonishing states through communal dance, forging a direct sense of cosmic belonging.

But if we can collectively support them —through initiatives that bolster land rights, cultural pride, language revitalization, and fair representation—we help ensure that a priceless piece of our collective heritage remains alive. We also ensure that curious seekers and dedicated researchers can continue to learn from the original wellsprings, not just from secondhand or commercialized versions. This is how we do justice to the "shamanic secrets" we so admire. We handle them with care, returning credit and resources to their rightful guardians, and letting the tradition speak for itself whenever possible. That might mean consulting actual San elders, or referencing local organizations that handle cultural affairs.

It might mean disclaiming that any adaptation we do is partial, gleaned from external observation, never fully replicating the real thing.

In the final analysis, the message is clear: the wisdom of the San spans from the deep past into the uncertain present, with gifts for anyone willing to honor it properly. It is not a closed system that says outsiders can never touch it, but it does demand reciprocity and understanding. We cannot simply watch a YouTube clip of a trance dance and declare ourselves experts. Nor can we wave around "n/um energy" as a new brand of self-help without context. We can, however, humbly open ourselves to the ways of communal healing, the interplay of myth, environment, and daily life, and the possibility that intangible worlds are always near at hand if we prepare ourselves through dance, chant, and the forging of a trusting circle.

The stance we adopt, then, is something like: "We see you, old ones, keepers of the first flame. Teach us, if you are willing, and we will do our best not to turn your gifts into cheap spectacle." Such an approach not only protects the integrity of the San practice but enriches us. Because in discovering the alchemy of the foot-stomping circle, we also see how we might heal ourselves. We see a method of addressing friction that does not revolve around endless debate or punishment, but around releasing negative energies through collective physical and spiritual exertion. We see a principle of leveling pride and sharing resources, so no one person's ego becomes toxic. We see a recognition that the natural environment is not a neutral backdrop but a living partner in the dance of life. All of these insights are extremely pertinent to a world grappling with ecological crises, mental health epidemics, and social fragmentation.

Such is the gift of the San. If, in the end, we can humbly receive that gift, we will find ourselves reattuned to rhythms older than any empire, older than any dogma or modern technology. We will recognize that the mightiest teacher could be a mantis deity who stumbles yet creates, or an Eland whose fat is deemed sacred for the transition into adulthood. We will remember that a small circle under the stars might hold more healing potential than we ever imagined. And perhaps we will step away from our pursuit of ephemeral distractions to find that in the simplicity of a shared dance, we can rediscover wholeness. This is what the San tradition has been whispering all along, through painted rocks and clicked consonants, through the half-death of the trance and the laughter that bursts forth as negativity is flung into the night.

In the end, a phrase in the /Xam tradition sometimes closes stories: "‖Khao-a, ‖ khao-a"—meaning "It is finished, it is done." We arrived at the conclusion of a journey, gleaning the broad outlines of how the San see life, how they harness the intangible realm, and how they continue to adapt in the face of modern disruptions. It is a concluding statement that acknowledges the circle completes yet the echo remains. So as we take our leave of this exploration, may we carry the resonance of the ancient Kalahari star-lore, the memory of communal healing as a possible future path, and the sense that each of us, in our own way, can reawaken a link to that first spark of human spirituality. May we hold the insights gleaned here not as a novelty but as seeds that can grow in our own contexts, always mindful to treat the source with the deepest respect. "Ke a h thank you" indeed, to the San for their example and to those who keep their flame burning bright. Let us bring that flame into our own hearts and kindle new fires of understanding wherever we go. The circle of the dance may pause, but the spirit of it—thrumming in dust, breath, and the hush before dawn—continues for those ready to listen.

Shakti Beauregard

References

Akroterion Journals. (n.d.). Various articles referencing |Kaggen or Cagn in Maloti San mythology and underground travel. Akroterion. Retrieved from http://akroterion.journals.ac.za

Biesele, M. (1993). Women like meat: The folklore and foraging ideology of the Kalahari Ju/'hoan. Witwatersrand University Press.

Bleek, W. H. I., & Lloyd, L. C. (1911). *Specimens of Bushman folklore*. G. Allen.

Blog Trainwrecklabs. (n.d.). Articles on San rock art, Matobo Hills cave paintings, and interpretations of oval/halo shapes. Retrieved from https://blog.trainwrecklabs.com

Britannica. (n.d.). *Aboriginal Dreamtime*. Encyclopedia Britannica. Retrieved from **https://www.britannica.com**

Britannica. (n.d.). *Rainbow Serpent*. Encyclopedia Britannica. Retrieved from **https://www.britannica.com**

Britannica. (n.d.). *Wandjina spirits*. Encyclopedia Britannica. Retrieved from **https://www.britannica.com**

Cultural Survival. (n.d.). *Ju/'hoan (!Kung) San*. Retrieved from https://www.culturalsurvival.org

Cultural Survival. (n.d.). *Land rights*. Retrieved from https://www.culturalsurvival.org

Course Hero. (n.d.). Mention of Ju/'hoansi or San healing dance references. Retrieved from **https://www.coursehero.com**

DuniArt. (n.d.). References to San cultural expressions, egalitarian ethos, and healing traditions. Retrieved from **https://duniart.com**

En.Wikipedia.org. (n.d.). Entries on Bushmen/San, Ancient Astronaut hypotheses, Fire-walking traditions, and other related topics. Retrieved from **https://en.wikipedia.org**

Encyclopedia Britannica. (n.d.). Entries on Aboriginal Dreamtime, Rainbow Serpent, Wandjina spirits, and other topics. Retrieved from **https://www.britannica.com**

Essex Myth. (n.d.). Articles discussing |Kaggen's creation of the first Eland, magical honey, and Mantis myths. Retrieved from https://essexmyth.wordpress.com

Feder, K. L. (2010). Encyclopedia of dubious archaeology: From Atlantis to the Walam Olum. Greenwood.

Gordon, R. (1992). The Bushman myth: The making of a Namibian Underclass. Westview Press.

Hitchcock, R. K., & Vinding, D. (Eds.). (2004). Indigenous peoples' rights in southern Africa. IWGIA.

Inner Traditions. (n.d.). Publications on Ju/'hoan healing dance, Katz & Biesele's works, and psychosocial benefits. Retrieved from https://www.innertraditions.com

JSTOR. (n.d.). Articles referencing David Lewis-Williams's interpretations of San rock art as trance imagery. Retrieved from https://www.jstor.org

Katz, R. (1982). Boiling energy: Community Healing among the Kalahari Kung. Harvard University Press.

Kruger Park. (n.d.). Descriptions of Eland significance in puberty rites and references to San dancing. Retrieved from https://www.krugerpark.co.za

Lee, R. B. (1968). What hunters do for a living, or, how to make out on scarce resources. In **R. B. Lee & I. DeVore** (Eds.), *Man the hunter* (pp. 30–48). Aldine.

Lee, R. B. (1979). The !Kung San: Men, women, and work in a foraging society. Cambridge University Press.

Lee, R. B. (2013). *The Dobe Ju/'hoansi* (4th ed.). Cengage Learning.

Lewis-Williams, J. D. (1981). Believing and seeing: Symbolic meanings in southern San rock paintings. Academic Press.

Lewis-Williams, J. D., & Dowson, T. A. (1989). Images of power: Understanding San Rock Art. Southern Book Publishers.

Marshall Thomas, E. (1959). *The harmless people*. Alfred A. Knopf.

Maypole of Wisdom. (n.d.). Discussing Bee myth (carrying Mantis), Blue Crane as |Kaggen's sister, Ostrich fire myths, etc. Retrieved from **https://maypoleofwisdom.com**

Phish.Net. (n.d.). Miscellaneous references to n/um & quotes describing "you dance, dance, dance… then n/um lifts you up Retrieved from **http://phish.net**

PubMed Central (PMC). (n.d.). Mentions of the !Kung "Giraffe Song" and healing dances in research contexts. Retrieved from **https://www.ncbi.nlm.nih.gov/pmc**

Reddit. (n.d.). Comparative mentions of Wandjina figures in Aboriginal art not being extraterrestrials. Retrieved from **https://www.reddit.com**

Reiters. (n.d.). Possibly referencing works by Katz, Biesele, or Ju/'hoan survival into the 21st century. Retrieved from https://www.reiters.com

Sacred Ecstatics. (n.d.). Articles on Ju/'hoan terminology like //xoan (heavy breathing) and "thread to God." Retrieved from https://www.sacredecstatics.com

South Africa Online. (n.d.). Articles on |Kaggen or Cagn, //Gaγa, creation myths, and other San beliefs. Retrieved from https://southafrica.co.za

Tishkoff, S. A., et al. (2009). The genetic structure and history of Africans and African Americans. *Science, 324*(5930), 1035–1044.

ThoughtCo. (n.d.). Content on San trance dance. Retrieved from https://www.thoughtco.com

ThoughtCo. (n.d.). *Content on Rain Dance*. Retrieved from https://www.thoughtco.com

Traill, A. (1978). The phonetic and phonological studies of Khoisan languages. *Khoisan Linguistic Studies, 4*, 29–42.

Wikipedia. (n.d.). Ancient Astronaut hypotheses. Retrieved from https://en.wikipedia.org

Wikipedia. (n.d.). *Bushmen/San*. Retrieved from https://en.wikipedia.org

Wikipedia. (n.d.). *Fire-walking traditions*. Retrieved from https://en.wikipedia.org

Thank you so much!

If you enjoyed this book, please **leave a review** on the marketplace you found the book in. This greatly helps our work and also **adds your voice** to the **renewed legacy** of the study of these **lost spiritual paths**.

For **more books** on spiritual paths, history, and mythology from Shakti Beauregard as well as other authors and publishers, please **scan the following QR code**:

…or **visit** www.mythological.center online!

© Copyright 2025 Beauregard Books
ISBN: 979-8-89760-027-4

www.ingramcontent.com/pod-product-compliance
Lightning Source LLC
LaVergne TN
LVHW051400080426
835508LV00022B/2906